BEOWULF

IN VERSE & IN PROSE

ROYAL
CLASSICS

Beowulf in Prose
Anonymous
Written in Anglo-Saxon c. 700 – 1000
Translated from Anglo-Saxon into Modern
   English Prose by Ernest J. B. Kirtlan
First Published by Charles H. Kelly in 1913

Beowulf in Verse
Anonymous
Translated from Anglo-Saxon into Modern
   English Verse by John Lesslie Hall
First Published by D. C. Heath & Co in 1892
Hall, John Lesslie 1856 – 1928
Text edits © 2024 Royal Classics
Design © 2024 Royal Classics

Cover design by: A.R. Roumanis

Text set in Minion Pro. Chapter headings
set in News Gothic Standard.

ISBN: 978-1-77878-468-2

FIRST EDITION / FIRST PRINTING

LIBRARY AND ARCHIVES CANADA CATALOGUING IN PUBLICATION

Title: Beowulf, in verse & in prose / prose, Ernest J.B. Kirtlan ; verse, John Lesslie Hall.
Other titles: Beowulf. English. | Beowulf, in verse and in prose | Container of (expression):
   Beowulf. English. (Kirtlan) | Container of (expression): Beowulf. English (Hall) 2024.
Names: Kirtlan, Ernest J. B. (Ernest John Brigham), translator. | Hall, J. Lesslie (John Lesslie),
   1856-1928, translator.
Description: First edition. | "Translated from Anglo-Saxon into modern
   English prose by Ernest J.B. Kirtlan; first published by Charles H. Kelly in 1913"--Copyright
   page. | "Translated from Anglo-Saxon into modern English verse by John Lesslie Hall; first
   published by D.C. Heath & Co in 1892"--Copyright page. | Text in English; translated from the
   Anglo-Saxon.
Identifiers: Canadiana 20240350499 | ISBN 9781778784682 (hardcover)
Subjects: LCSH: Beowulf—Translations into English. | LCGFT: Epic poetry.
Classification: LCC PR1583 .K47 2024 | DDC 829/.3—DC23

BEOWULF
IN VERSE & IN PROSE

PROSE
Ernest J. B. Kirtlan

VERSE
John Lesslie Hall

VANCOUVER:
ROYAL CLASSICS
2024

CONTENTS

BEOWULF
IN PROSE

Ernest J. B. Kirtlan

NOTE AS TO USE OF APPENDIX

I HAVE RELEGATED to the Appendix all notes of any considerable length. The reader is advised to consult the Appendices wherever directed in the footnotes. He will then have a much clearer conception of the principal characters and events of the poem.

INTRODUCTION

'BEOWULF' MAY RIGHTLY be pronounced the great national epic of the Anglo-Saxon race. Not that it exalts the race so much as that it presents the spirit of the Anglo-Saxon peoples, the ideals and aims, the manners and customs, of our ancestors, and that it does so in setting before us a great national hero. Beowulf himself was not an Anglo-Saxon. He was a Geat-Dane; but he belonged to that confraternity of nations that composed the Teutonic people. He lived in an heroic age, when the songs of the wandering singers were of the great deeds of outstanding men. The absolute epic of the English people has yet to be written. To some extent Arthur, though a British King – that is to say, though he was King of the Celtic British people, who were subsequently driven into the West, into Cornwall and Wales and Strathclyde, by our Saxon ancestors – became nationalized by our Anglo-Norman ancestors as a typical King of the English people. He has become the epic King of the English in the poetry of Tennyson. It is always a mystery to the writer that no competent singer among us has ever laid hands upon our own Saxon hero, King Alfred. It is sometimes said that there is nothing new under the sun, that there is nothing left for the modern singer to sing about, and that the realm of possible musical production is fast vanishing out of view. Certainly this is not true of poetry. Both Alfred and Arthur are waiting for the sympathetic voice that will tell forth to the world the immortal splendour of their personalities. And just as the Anglo-Normans idealized Arthur as a hero-king of the English nation, though he really fought against the English, so the Saxon singer of Beowulf has idealized this Geatish chieftain, and in some way set him forth as the idealized chieftain of the Teutonic race.

Beowulf is an Anglo-Saxon poem. – It consists of 3182 lines. It is written in the alliterative verse of our ancestors in the Anglo-Saxon tongue, which, though the mother-tongue of the English, is yet more difficult to read for the Englishman than Latin or Greek. One wonders whether any genuine Anglo-Saxon epic existed, and has been destroyed in the passing of the centuries. The curious feature about this poem is that it concerns a man who was not an Anglo-Saxon. Our poem is written in the West Saxon dialect. The original poem was probably in Northumbrian, and was translated into West Saxon during the period of literary efflorescence in the West Saxon Court. We do not know whether it was a translation or whether it was original, though the latter is, I believe, the prevailing opinion. Arnold has put forth what may be called the missionary theory of its origin. He believes that both the choice of subject and the grade of culture may be connected with the missionary efforts of the English Church of those days to extend Christianity in Friesland and further east. 'It does not seem improbable that it was in the interest of the spread of Christianity that the composer of *Beowulf* – perhaps a missioner, perhaps a layman attached to the mission – was attracted to the Scandinavian lands; that he resided there long enough to become thoroughly steeped in the folk-lore and local traditions; that he found the grand figure of Beowulf the Geat predominant in them; and that, weaving into an organic whole those which he found suitable to his own purpose, he composed an epic which, on his return home, must soon have become known to all the lovers of English song.'[1] Dr. Sarrazin thought this unknown poet might have been the famous Cynewulf. Arnold, chiefly on stylistic grounds, differs from this opinion. This is Arnold's opinion: 'Sagas, either in the Danish dialect or that of the Geats – more probably the latter – were current in the Scandinavian countries in the seventh century. Among these sagas, that of Beowulf the Geat must have had a prominent place; others celebrated Hygelac his uncle, Hnaef the Viking, the wars of the Danes and the Heathobards, of the Danes and the Swedes. About the end of the century missionaries from England are known to have been busy in Friesland and Denmark, endeavouring to convert the natives to Christianity. Some one of these, whose mind had a turn for literature and dwelt with joy upon the traditions of the past, collected or learnt by heart a number of these sagas, and, taking that of *Beowulf* as a basis, and weaving some others into his work, composed an epic poem to which, although it contains the record of those adventures, the heroic scale of the figure who accomplishes them all imparts a real unifying epic interest.' Whatever may be the truth as to its origin, there it lies in the British Museum in its unique MS. as a testimony to all ages of the genius of the Anglo-Saxon race.

1   See Arnold, p. 115.?

Now it will be quite naturally asked, What do we learn from *Beowulf* of the genius and spirit of that race from which we are sprung?

The one outstanding fact, as it appears to the writer, is the co-operative principle. And this principle stands in almost violent opposition to the ruling principle of the modern world, in which society is divided into a number of mutually opposite sections or classes, whose interests clash with fatal results to individual and corporate well-being. In this poem we see the whole community, from the King to the churl, bound by one common interest. King and chieftain and thane and churl freely intermingle and converse. They eat and drink and sleep under one common roof, or at least in one common enclosure. *Tempora mutantur*! but the idea of social interaction and mutual interdependence never found more vivid or real expression than in the pictures presented in *Beowulf* of Hart, the Great Hall of Hrothgar, and in the Court and township of Hygelac, King of the Geats. In the Hall of Hart Hrothgar and his Queen and his courtiers sit at the high table on the dais, and the lower orders at the long table down the hall. The spears and shields adorn the walls. After the evening meal, the singer, or scop, as he is called, to the accompaniment of the harp, tells forth the deeds of some ancient feud, such as that of Finn and the Danes or the Fight at Finnsburgh, or the feud of the Danes and the Heathobards, in which Freawaru, Hrothgar's daughter, and Ingeld figure so tragically. Then the benches are removed, and the rude beds are spread out on the floor of the Great Hall and they seek 'evening rest.' The whole is a picture of fraternal and paternal government. If Grendel, the Fen-monster, carries away one of their number, then there is weeping and lamentation. The King and the Queen and the nobility and the commonalty are all concerned in the tragedy. The loss of one is the loss of all. When Aeschere is slain by Grendel's mother Hrothgar thus bewails his loss: 'Seek no more after joy; sorrow is renewed for the Danish folk. Aeschere is dead, he who was my wise counsellor and my adviser and my comrade in arms, when in time of war we defended ourselves; ... but now the hand lieth low which bestowed every kind of joy upon you.' And in the end of the poem it is said of Beowulf that he was 'most gentle to his folk.' The King was king only 'for his folk.' The interest of his folk, their physical and moral well-being, was his chief solicitude.

2. But not only was this so within any one nation or tribe, but there was a sense of comradeship and mutual responsibility among those of various tribes and nations. When Beowulf the Geat hears in Gautland of the raids of Grendel upon Hart, he commands his folk to make ready a boat that he may fare across the sea to the help of Hrothgar, because

'he was lacking in warriors.' Beowulf's whole mission in Hart was the discharge of a solemn obligation of help from the strong to the weak. He announces to Hrothgar that he is come 'to cleanse Hart of ill,' and this he feels he *must* do. 'Woe is me if I preach not the gospel!' cried St. Paul. 'Woe is me if I help not the weak and cleanse not the demon-infested palace of my kinsman!' cried Beowulf. 'Weird goes as he willeth'; that is, Fate must be submitted to. And Fate hath willed that he should help the weak and 'cleanse the ill.'

3. Then there is the tremendous sense of loyalty on the part of the folk to their king or chieftain. The idea of the 'Comitatus' bound the folk to their leaders. Nothing more disgraceful could be conceived than the desertion of the leader. Terrible were the reproaches hurled at the trembling cowards who had hurried away into the woods, to save their own skins, whilst their King Beowulf wrestled with the dragon, the enemy of the people. 'Yea, death is better for any earl than a life of reproach.' Loyalty, a passionate loyalty to the King, was the greatest of virtues, and disloyalty and cowardice the greatest of vices. Society was an organic whole, bound together by the bands of loyalty and devotion to the common good.

4. There is, too, the fatalistic note heard all through the poem. Beowulf feels himself hard pressed by Fate. The Anglo-Saxon called Fate by the name 'Weird,' which has survived in modern English in the sense of something strange and mysterious. Weird was the God, or Goddess of Fate. Again and again in the poem we hear the solemn, minor, dirge-like refrain, 'Weird hath willed it'; 'Goeth Weird as she willeth' (chapter VI. p. 44). There is this perpetual overshadowing and almost crushing sense of some inscrutable and irresistible power that wieldeth all things and disposeth all things, which is, I believe, a pre-eminent characteristic of the Anglo-Saxon race, and accounts for the dare-devil courage of her sons upon the battle-field or on the high seas. We find it, too, in its morally less attractive form in the recrudescent pessimism of modern literature. Thomas Hardy is the lineal descendant in literature of the author of *Beowulf* when he says: 'Thus the President of the Immortals had finished his sport with poor Tess.'[2]

5. And closely allied to this sense of Destiny is the sombre view of life that is characteristic of the Teutonic peoples. There is none of that passionate joy in beauty and in love that we find in the Celtic literature. Life is a serious thing in *Beowulf* and with us of the Anglo-Saxon race. The scenery of *Beowulf* is massive and threatening and mist-en-

2   See conclusion of Tess of the D'Urbervilles?

circled. Angry seas are boiling and surging and breaking at the foot of lofty and precipitous cliffs. Above the edge of the cliffs stretch mysterious and gloomy moorlands, and treacherous bogs and dense forests inhabited by malignant and powerful spirits, the foes of humanity. In a land like this there is no time for love-making. Eating, drinking, sleeping, fighting there make up the business of life. It is to the Celtic inflow that we owe the addition of love in our modern literature. The composer of *Beowulf* could not have conceived the Arthur Saga or the Tristram love-legend. These things belong to a later age, when Celtic and Teutonic elements were fused in the Anglo-Norman race. But we still find in our literature the sombre hues. And, after all, it is in the forest of sorrow and pain that we discover the most beautiful flowers and the subtlest perfumes.

I desire to express my indebtedness to A. J. Wyatt and William Morris for their translations; to A. J. Wyatt for his edition of the poem in the original; to Thomas Arnold for his terse and most informing work on *Beowulf*; to the authors of articles in the *Encyclopaedia Britannica* and in Chambers's *Encyclopaedia and The Cambridge History of English Literature*.

Ernest J. B. Kirtlan.

Brighton,

November, 1913.

THE PRELUDE

Now we have heard, by inquiry, of the glory of the kings of the people, they of the Spear-Danes, how the Athelings were doing deeds of courage.[1] Full often Scyld, the son of Scef, with troops of warriors, withheld the drinking-stools from many a tribe. This earl caused terror when at first he was found in a miserable case. Afterwards he gave help when he grew up under the welkin, and worshipfully he flourished until all his neighbours over the sea gave him obedience, and yielded him tribute. He was a good king. In after-time there was born to him a son in the Court, whom God sent thither as a saviour of the people. He saw the dire distress that they formerly suffered when for a long while they were without a prince. Then it was that the Lord of Life, the Wielder of glory, gave to him glory. Famous was Beowulf.[2] Far and wide spread his fame. Heir was he of Scyld in the land of the Danes. Thus should a young man be doing good deeds, with rich gifts to the friends of his father, so that in later days, when war shall come upon them, boon companions may stand at his side, helping their liege lord. For in all nations, by praiseworthy deeds, shall a man be thriving.

At the fated hour Scyld passed away, very vigorous in spirit, to the keeping of his Lord. Then his pleasant companions carried him down to the ocean flood, as he himself had bidden them, whilst the friend of the Scyldings was wielding words, he who as the dear Lord of the Land had ruled it a long time. And there, in the haven, stood the ship, with rings at the prow, icy, and eager for the journey, the ferry of the Atheling.

Then they laid down their dear Lord the giver of rings, the famous man, on the bosom of the ship, close to the mast, where were heaps

1   See Appendix II.?
2   Not the hero of the poem.?

of treasures, armour trappings that had been brought from far ways. Never heard I of a comelier ship, decked out with battle-weapons and weeds of war, with swords and byrnies. In his bosom they laid many a treasure when he was going on a far journey, into the power of the sea. Nor did they provide for him less of booty and of national treasures than they had done, who at the first had sent him forth, all alone o'er the waves, when he was but a child. Then moreover they set a golden standard high o'er his head, and let the sea take him, and gave all to the man of the sea. Full sad were their minds, and all sorrowing were they. No man can say soothly, no, not any hall-ruler, nor hero under heaven, who took in that lading.[3]

3   Cp. with this the 'Passing of Arthur,' as related by Tennyson. The meaning is clear. Cp. also Appendix.?

The Story

ONE

MOREOVER the Danish Beowulf,[1] the dear King of his people, was a long time renowned amongst the folk in the cities (his father, the Prince, had gone a-faring elsewhere from this world). Then was there born to him a son, the high Healfdene; and while he lived he was ruling the happy Danish people, and war-fierce and ancient was he. Four children were born to him: Heorogar the leader of troops, and Hrothgar, and Halga the good. And I heard say that Queen Elan (wife of Ongentheow) was his daughter, and she became the beloved comrade of the Swede. Then to Hrothgar was granted good speed in warfare and honour in fighting, so that his loyal subjects eagerly obeyed him, until the youths grew doughty, a very great band of warriors. Then it burned in his mind that he would bid men be building a palace, a greater mead-hall than the children of men ever had heard of, and that he would therein distribute to young and to old, as God gave him power, all the wealth that he had save the share of the folk and the lives of men.

Then I heard far and wide how he gave commandment to many a people throughout all the world, this work to be doing, and to deck out the folkstead. In due time it happened that soon among men, this greatest of halls was now all ready. And Hart he called it, whose word had great wielding. He broke not his promise, but gave to them rings and treasures at the banquet. The hall towered on high, and the gables were wide between the horns,[2] and awaited the surging of the loath-

---

1   Not the hero of this poem.?
2   The gables were decorated with horns of stags and other beasts of the chase.?

some flames. Not long time should pass ere hatred was awakened after the battle-slaughter, twixt father-in-law and son-in-law.[3]

Then it was that the powerful sprite who abode in darkness, scarce could brook for a while that daily he heard loud joy in the hall. There was sound of harping, and the clear song of the bard.

He who knew it was telling of the beginning of mankind, and he said that the Almighty created the world, and the bright fields surrounded by water. And, exulting, He set the sun and the moon as lamps to shine upon the earth-dwellers, and adorned the world with branches and leaves. And life He was giving to every kind of living creature. So noble men lived in joy, and were all blessed till one began to do evil, a devil from hell; and this grim spirit was called Grendel. And he was a march-stepper, who ruled on the moorlands, the fens, and the stronghold. For a while he kept guard, this unhappy creature, over the land of the race of monsters, since the Creator had proscribed him. On the race of Cain the Eternal Lord brought death as vengeance, when he slew Abel. Nor did he find joy in the feud, but God for the crime drove him far thence. Thus it was that evil things came to their birth, giants and elves and monsters of the deep, likewise those giants who for a long while were striving with God Himself. And well He requited them.

---

3   See Appendix V., and chapters XXVIII, and XXIX.?

TWO

THEN HE WENT visiting the high house after nightfall, to see how the Ring-Danes were holding it. And he found there a band of Athelings asleep after feasting. And they knew not sorrow or the misery of men. The grim and greedy wight of destruction, all fierce and furious, was soon ready for his task, and laid hold of thirty thanes, all as they lay sleeping. And away he wended, faring homeward and exulting in the booty, to revisit his dwellings filled full of slaughter. At the dawn of day the war-craft of Grendel was seen by men. Then after his feeding they set up a weeping, great noise in the morning.

The glorious Lord, the very good Atheling, sat all unblithely, and suffered great pain, and endured sorrow for his thanes, when they saw the track of the loathly one, the cursed sprite. That struggle was too strong, loathsome and long. And after but one night (no longer time was it) he did them more murder-bale, and recked not a whit the feud and the crime. Too quick was he therein. Then he who had sought elsewhere more at large a resting-place, a bed after bower, was easily found when he was shown and told most truly, by the token so clear, the hate of the hell-thane. He went away farther and faster, he who would escape the fiend. So he ruled and strove against right, he alone against all of them, until the best of houses stood quite idle. And a great while it was – the friend of the Danes suffered distress and sorrows that were great the time of twelve winters.

Then was it made known to the children of men by a sorrowful singing that Grendel was striving this while against Hrothgar, and waged hateful enmity of crime and feud for many a year with lasting strife, and would hold no truce against any man of the main host of Danes, nor put away the life-bale, or settle feud with a fee, nor did any man need to hope for brighter bettering at the hand of the banesman. The terrible monster, a dark death-shadow, was pursuing the youth and the warriors, and he fettered and ensnared them, and ever was holding night after night the misty moorlands. And, men know not ever whither workers of hell-runes wander to and fro. Thus the foe of mankind, the terrible and lonesome traveller, often he did them even greater despite. And he took up his dwelling in the treasure-decked Hall of Hart in the dark night, nor could he come near the throne the treasure of God, nor did he know His love.[4]

And great was the evil to the friend of the Danes, and breakings of heart. Many a strong one sat in council, and much they discussed what was best for stout-hearted men to do against the fearful terror. And sometimes they went vowing at their heathen shrines and offered sacrifices, and with many words pleaded that the devil himself would give them his help against this menace to the nation. For such was their custom, the hope of the heathen. And ever of Hell they thought in their hearts; the Creator they knew not, the Judge of all deeds, nor knew they the Lord God, nor could they worship the Protector of the heavens, the Wielder of glory. Woe be to that man who shall shove down a soul through hurtful malice into the bosom of the fire, and who hopes for no help nor for any change – well shall it be with that one who after his death day shall seek the Lord and desire protection in the embrace of the Father.

4   Wyatt's translation of 'Ne his myne wisse.'?

THREE

So Beowulf, son of Healfdene, ever was brooding over this time-care, nor could the brave hero avert woe. That conflict was too strong, loathsome and long, that terrible and dire distress, the greatest of night-bales which came to the people.

Then the thane of Hygelac,[5] the good man of the Geats,[6] heard from home of the deeds of Grendel. And on the day of this life he was the strongest of main of all men in the world; noble was he and powerful. He bade a fair ship be made, and said that he would be seeking the War-King, the famous prince, over the swan path, and that he needed men. And the proud churls little blamed him for that journey, though dear he was to them. They urged on the valiant man and marked the omen. The good man of the Geats had chosen champions of those who were keenest, and sought out the ship. And one, a sea-crafty man, pointed to the land-marks. Time passed by; the ship was on the waves, the boat under the cliff, and the warriors all readily went up to the stern. And the currents were swirling, with sea and sand. And men were carrying on to the naked deck bright ornaments and splendid war-armour. Then they shove forth the ship that was well bound together; and it set forth over the waves, driven by the wind, this foamy-necked ship, likest to a bird; until about the same time on the next day, the ship with its twisted stern had gone so far that the sailing men could see the land, the shining sea-cliffs, the steep mountains, and the wide sea-nesses. Then they crossed the remaining portion of the sea.[7] The Geats went up quickly on to the shore, and anchored the ship. War-shirts and war-weeds were rattling. And they gave God thanks for their easy crossing of the waves. Then the ward of the Swedes, who kept guard over the sea-cliffs, saw them carry down the gangways the bright shields and armour, all ready. And full curious thought tortured him as to who these men were. He, the thane of Hrothgar, rode down to the beach on his charger, and powerfully brandished the spear in his hand and took counsel with them.

---

5 i.e. Beowulf.?
6 Geats. The tribe to which Beowulf belonged. They inhabited southern Sweden between the Danes on the south and the Swedes on the north. See Appendix XI.?
7 Literally, 'Then was the sea traversed at the end of the ocean.'?

'Who are ye armour-bearers, protected by byrnies, who come here thus bringing the high vessel over the sea, and the ringed ship over the ocean? I am he that sits at the end of the land and keep sea-guard, so that no one more loathsome may scathe with ship-army the land of the Danes. Never have shield-bearers begun to come here more openly, yet ye seem not to know the password of warriors, the compact of kinsmen. Nor ever have I seen a greater earl upon earth, than one of your band, a warrior in armour. And except his face belie him, he that is thus weapon-bedecked is no hall-man; but a peerless one to see. Now must I know your lineage before you go farther with your false spies in the land of the Danes. Now O ye far-dwellers and sea-farers, hear my onefold thought – haste is best in making known whence ye are come.'

FOUR

THEN THE ELDEST GAVE answer, and unlocked his treasure of words, the wise one of the troop: 'We are of the race of the Geats and hearth-comrades of Hygelac. My father was well known to the folk, a noble prince was he called Ecgtheow. And he bided many winters, ere as an old man he set out on his journeys away from the dwelling places. And wellnigh every councillor throughout all the world remembered him well. We through bold thinking have come to seek thy lord, the son of Healfdene, the protector of the people. Vouchsafe to us good guid-ance. We have a great business with the lord of the Danes, who is far famed. Nor of this shall aught be secret as I am hoping. Well thou knowest if 'tis true as we heard say, that among the Danes some secret evil-doer, I know not what scather, by terror doth work unheard-of hostility, humiliation, and death. I may give counsel through great-ness of mind to Hrothgar as to how he, the wise and good, may over-come the fiend, if ever should cease for him the baleful business and bettering come after and his troubles wax cooler, or for ever he shall suffer time of stress and miserable throes, while the best of all houses shall remain on the high stead.'

Then the watchman, the fearless warrior, as he sat on his horse, quickly made answer: 'The shield-warrior who is wide awake, shall know how to tell the difference between words and works, if he well bethink him. I can see that this band of warriors will be very welcome to the Lord of the Danes. Go ye forth, therefore, bear weapons and armour, as I will direct you. And I will command my thanes to hold against every foe, your ship in honour, new tarred as it is, and dry on the sands, until it shall carry the dearly loved man, that ship with the twisted prow, to the land of the Geats. To each of the well-doers shall it be given to escape scot-free out of the battle rush.' Then they went forth carrying their weapons. And there the ship rested, fastened by a rope, the wide-bosomed vessel secured by its anchor. The Boar[8] held life ward, bright and battle-hard and adorned with gold, over the neck-guard of the handsome Beowulf. There was snorting of the war-like-

---

8   Frequent references are made to the device of the boar on shield and helmet; cp. p. 77, in description of Hnaef's funeral pyre.?

minded, whilst men were hastening, as they marched on together till they caught sight of the splendid place decked out in gold. And it was the most famous of palaces, under the heavens, of the earth-dwellers, where the ruler was biding. Its glory shone over many lands. Then the dear one in battle showed them the bright house where were the brave ones, that they might straightway make their way towards it. Then one of the warriors turned his horse round, and spake this word: 'Time it is for me to go. May the Almighty Father hold you in favour, and keep you in safety in all your journeyings. I will go to the sea-coast to keep my watch against the fierce troops.'

FIVE

THE WAY WAS PAVED with many coloured stones, and by it they knew the path they should take. The coat of mail shone brightly, which was firmly hand-locked. The bright iron ring sang in the armour as they came on their way in their warlike trappings at the first to the great hall. Then the sea-weary men set down their broad shields, their shields that were wondrous hard 'gainst the wall of the great house, and bowed towards the bench. And byrnies were rattling, the war-weapons of men. And the spears were standing in a row together, the weapons of the sea-men and the spear grey above. And the troop of armed men was made glorious with weapons. Then the proud chieftain asked the warriors of their kindred: 'From whence are ye bringing such gold-plated shields, grey sarks and helmets with visors, and such a heap of spears? I am the servant and messenger of Hrothgar. Never saw I so many men prouder. I trow it was for pride and not at all for banishment, but for greatness of mind that Hrothgar ye are seeking.'

Then answered the brave man, the chief of the Geats, and spake these words, hard under helmet: 'We are the comrades at table of Hygelac. Beowulf is my name. I will say fully this my errand to the son of Healfdene the famous chieftain, unto thy lord and master, if he will grant us that we may salute him who is so good.'

Then spake Wulfgar (he was Prince of the Wendels[9]). His courage was known to all, his valour and wisdom. 'I will make known to the Prince of the Danes, the Lord of the Scyldings[10] the giver of rings the famous chieftain as thou art pleading, about thy journey, and will make known to thee quickly the answer which he the good man thinks fit to give me.' Quickly he turned then to where Hrothgar was sitting, old and very grey with his troop of earls. The brave man then went and stood before the shoulders of the Lord of the Danes. Well he knew the custom of the doughty ones. Wulfgar then spoke to his lord and friend: 'Here are come faring from a far country over the wide sea, a people of the Geats, and the eldest the warriors call Beowulf. And they are asking that they may exchange words with thee, my lord. O gladman Hroth-

---

9   The name of a reigning Danish dynasty.?
10   For Scyld cp. Appendix II.?

gar, do not refuse to be talking with them. For worthy they seem all in their war-weeds, in the judgement of earls. At least he is a daring Prince who hither hath led this band of warriors.'

SIX

THEN SPAKE HROTHGAR THE protector of the Danes: 'Well I knew him when he was a child, and his old father was called Ecgtheow. And to him did Hrethel of the Geats give his only daughter, and his son is bravely come here and hath sought out a gracious friend.' Then said the sea-farers who had brought the goodly gifts of the Geats there for thanks, that he the battle-brave had in his hand-grip the main craft of thirty men. 'And the holy God hath sent him for favour to us West Danes, and of this I have hope, 'gainst the terror of Grendel. I shall offer the goodman gifts for his daring. Now make thou haste and command the band of warrior kinsmen into the presence. Bid them welcome to the people of the Danes.' Then went Wulfgar even to the hall-door, and spake these words: 'My liege lord, the Prince of the East Danes, commands me to say that he knows your lineage. And ye who are bold of purpose are welcome hither over the sea-waves. Now may ye go in your war-weeds, under your visored helmets to see Hrothgar. Let your swords stay behind here, the wood and the slaughter-shafts and the issue of words.' Then the Prince rose up, and about him was many a warrior, a glorious band of thanes. And some bided there and held the battle-garments as the brave man commanded. And they hastened together under the roof of Hrothgar as the man directed them. The stout-hearted man went forward, hard under helmet till he stood by the dais.

Then Beowulf spake (and the byrny shone on him, the coat of mail, sewn by the cunning of the smith): 'O Hrothgar, all hail! I am the kinsman and comrade of Hygelac.[11] Many marvels I have set on foot in the days of my youth. The affair of Grendel was made known to me in my native land. Sea-farers told how this best of all palaces stood idle and useless to warriors, after evening light came down under the brightness of heaven. Then my people persuaded me, the best and the proudest of all my earls, O my lord Hrothgar, that I should seek thee, for they well knew my main strength. For they themselves saw how I came forth bloodstained from the power of the fiend, when I bound the five, and destroyed the giant's kin, and slew 'mongst the waves, sea-monsters by night, and suffered such dire distress, and wreaked vengeance for

---

11   Hygelac, King of the Geats at the time, and uncle of Beowulf.?

the strife of the Geats (for woe they were suffering), and I destroyed the fierce one. And now all alone I shall settle the affair of Grendel the deadly monster, the cruel giant. And one boon will I be asking, O Prince of the Bright Danes, thou lord of the Scyldings, Protector of warriors and friend of the folk, that thou wilt not refuse, since so far I am come, that I and my troop of earls, this crowd of brave men, may alone cleanse out Hart. I have heard say also that the monster because of his rashness recks not of weapons. And, if Hygelac the blithe-minded will be my liege lord, I will forgo to carry to the battle a sword, or broad shield all yellow; but I will engage by my hand-grip with the enemy, and strive for life, foe with foe. And he whom Death taketh shall believe in the doom of the Lord. And I doubt not he will fearlessly consume the people of the Geats, if he may prevail in the war-hall as he has often done with the strong men of the Danes. And thou shalt not need to hide my head if Death take me, for he will seize me all bloodstained, and will bury the slaughter all bloody, and will think to taste and devour me alone and without any sorrow, and will stain the glens in the moorland. And thou needest not to sorrow longer over the food of my body. And if battle take me, send to Hygelac this best of coats of mail, the noblest of garments. It is the heirloom of Hrethel the work of Weland[12]; and let Weird go as it will.'

---

12   Weland – 'the famous smith of Germanic legend,' says Wyatt – who also refers us to the Franks Casket in the British Museum.?

SEVEN

HROTHGAR GAVE ANSWER, the protector of the Danes: 'O my friend Beowulf, now thou hast sought us, for defence and for favour. Thy father fought in the greatest of feuds. He was banesman to Heatholaf amongst the Wylfings, when for battle-terror the King of the Geats could not hold him. Thence he sought the folk of the South Danes over the welter of waves. Then first was I ruling the Danish folk, and in my youthful days possessed the costly jewels, the treasure city of heroes. Then Heregar was dead, my elder brother not living was he, the child of Healfdene. He was a better man than I was. Then a payment of money settled the matter. I sent to the Wylfings ancient presents over the sea-ridges. And he swore to me oaths. And it is to me great sorrow in my heart to tell any man what Grendel hath done in Hart through his malice, of humiliation and sudden horror. My hall-troop has grown less, the crowd of my thanes; Weird[13] has swept them towards the terror of Grendel. But easily may the good God restrain the deeds of the foolish scather. And drunken with beer the warriors full often boasted o'er the ale-cup that they would bide in the beer-hall the battle of Grendel with the terror of swords. Then was the mead-hall all bloodstained in the morning when dawn came shining, and all the benches were wet with gore, the hall with sword-blood. And so much the less did I rule o'er dear doughty ones whom death had taken. Now sit down to the banquet and unbind thy thoughts, thy hopes to the thanes, as thy mind inspires thee.' Then was there room made in the beer-hall for the Geats all together. And there they went and sat down, the strong-hearted men, proud of their strength. And a thane waited on them, who bore in his hands the ale-cup bedecked, and he poured out the sparkling mead, while the clear-voiced bard kept singing in Hart. There was joy to the heroes, and a very great gathering of Danes and of Geats.

---

13   Weird was a peculiarly English conception. It means Fate, or Destiny. Then Weird became a god or goddess – cp. 'The Seafarer,' an Old English poem in which we find 'Weird is stronger, the Lord is mightier than any man's thoughts.'?

EIGHT

SPAKE THEN UNFERTH, the son of Eglaf, who sat at the feet of the Lord of the Danes and opened a quarrel. (For the journey of Beowulf, of the brave sea-farer, was vexation to him, for he could not brook that ever any other man than he himself should obtain greater fame in all the earth.)

'What!' said he, 'art thou that Beowulf who didst contend with Breca, and strovest for the mastery in swimming o'er wide seas, when ye two for pride were searching the waves and for foolish boasting risked your lives in the deep waters? No man could dissuade you from that sorrowful journey, neither friend nor foe, when ye two swam in the sea, when ye two enfolded the waves with your arms and measured the sea-ways and brandished your arms as you glided o'er the ocean. The sea boiled with waves the wintry whelming. And for seven nights long ye were toiling in the stress of seas. But he o'erpowered thee in swimming, for greater strength had he. Then at the morning tide the sea bore him up to the land of the Heathoremes. Thence he was seeking the friend of his people his own dear country, the land of the Brondings, the fair city of refuge, where he had his own folk, and a city and rings. The son of Beanstan soothly fulfilled his boasting against thee. So do I deem it a worse matter, though thou art everywhere doughty in the rush of battle and grim warfare, if thou shalt be daring to bide near Grendel a night-long space.'

Then Beowulf spake, the son of Ecgtheow: 'What! my friend Unferth, drunken with beer, many things thou art saying about that Breca and talkest of his journey. But soothly I tell thee that I had the greater strength in that swimming, and endurance in the waves. We two agreed when we were youngsters, and boasted (for we were both still in the days of our youth) that we in the ocean would be risking our lives. And so in deed we did. We had a naked sword hard in our hands when we were swimming. We two were thinking to guard us 'gainst whale fishes. Nor over the sea-waves might he be floating a whit far from me, more quickly on the waters. Then we together were in the sea for the space of five nights until the flood, the boiling waters drove us asunder. And the coldest of weather, and the darkening night, and a wind from the north battle-grim turned against us, and rough were the waves. And the mind of the mere-fishes was stirred when my shirt of mail that was hand-locked gave to me help against the foe. The decorated battle-robe lay on my breast all adorned with gold, and the doomÈd and dire foe drew to the bottom, and fast he had me grim in his grip. Still to me was granted that I reached to the monster with the point of my sword. And the mighty sea-deer carried off the battle-rush through my hand.'

NINE

'So then evil-doers did often oppress me. And I served them with my dear sword as was most fitting. Not at all of the feasting had they any joy. Evil destroyers sat round the banquet at the bottom of the sea, that they might seize me. But in the morning, wounded by my sword, they lay up on the foreshore, put to sleep by my weapon so that they hindered no more the faring of the sea-goers. Light came from the east-ward, the bright beacon of God. The waves grew less that I could catch sight of the sea-nesses, the windy walls. Weird often saveth the earl that is undoomed when his courage is doughty. Nevertheless it happened that I slew with my sword nine of the sea-monsters. Nor have I heard under vault of heaven of a harder night-struggle, nor of a more wretch-ed man on the sea-streams. Still I escaped from the grasp of the foes, with my life, and weary of the journey. When the sea bore me up, on the flood tide, on the welling of waves, to the land of the Finns. Nor have I heard concerning thee of any such striving or terror of swords. Breca never yet, nor either of you two, did such a deed with shining sword in any battle-gaming (not that I will boast of this too much), yet wast thou the slayer of thy brother, thy chief kinsman. And for this in hell shalt thou suffer a curse, though thy wit be doughty. And soothly I tell thee, O son of Eglaf, that Grendel that hateful monster never had done such terrors to thy life and humiliation in Hart if thy mind and thy soul were as battle-fierce as thou thyself dost say. But he has found that he needed not to fear the feud the terrible sword-thrust of your people the Danes. He taketh forced toll, and spareth none of the Danish people, but joyfully wageth war, putteth them to sleep and feedeth on them, and expecteth no fight from the Danes. But I shall ere long offer him in war the strength and the courage of the Geats. Let him go who can to the mead all proudly when morning light shall shine from the south, another day over the children of men.'

Then in the hall the giver of rings was grey-haired and battle-brave. The Prince of the Danes was hopeful of help. The guardian of the folk fixed on Beowulf his firm-purposed thought. There was laughter 'mong heroes, din resounded, and words were winsome. Wealtheow went forth, the Queen of Hrothgar, mindful of kinship and decked out in gold, she greeted Beowulf in the hall. And then the lovely wife first proffered the goblet to the Lord of the East Danes, and bade him be blithe at the beer-drinking, he who was dear to all his people. And gladly he took the banquet and hall-cup, he the victorious King. The lady of the Helmings[14] went round about every one of the youthful warriors, and proffered the costly cup, until the time came that the ring-adorned Queen, most excellent in spirit, bore the mead-cup then to Beowulf. She, the wise in words, greeted the Geats and gave thanks to God that she had her desire that she might trust in any earl for help against such crimes. He gladly received it, he the battle-fierce warrior, from the hand of Wealtheow, and then began singing, inspired by a warlike spirit.

Beowulf spake, the son of Ecgtheow: 'I had intended at once to work out the will of this your people when I set forth over the sea and sat in my sea-boat with the troop of my people, or that I would fall in the slaughter fast in the fiend's grip. I shall yet acquit myself as befitteth an earl, or in the mead-hall await my last day.' And well the lady liked the words, the boasting of the Geat. And that lovely queen went all decked out in gold to sit by her lord. Then mighty words were spoken in the hall as before, by the people in joyance and the noise of the victors, until the son of Healfdene[15] straightway would be seeking his evening rest. And he knew that a battle was doomed in the high hall to the monster when no longer they could see the light of the sun, or darkening night came stalking over all the shapes of shadows. The troop of warriors rose up, the Lord greeted the other, Hrothgar greeted Beowulf, and wished him good health and the warding of that wine-hall, and he spake the word: 'Since the time that I could lift my hand or my shield, never have I given the mighty hall of the Danes into the care of any, except now to thee. Have now and hold thou this best of houses, be thou mindful of honour, and show thyself courageous, and wakeful 'gainst foes. Nor shalt thou lack joy if thou escapest from that brave work with life.'

14 i.e. Wealtheow, Hrothgar's Queen, who was of this tribe.?
15 Healfdene was the father of Hrothgar, King of the Danes.?

TEN

THEN HROTHGAR DEPARTED WITH his troop of heroes, he the Prince of the Scyldings; out of Hall went he, for the battle-chieftain would be seeking out Wealtheow his Queen, that they might go to rest. The glory of kings had appointed a hall-ward, as men say, against Grendel. A thane was in waiting on the Prince of the Danes, and his watch was keeping against the giant. The Lord of the Geats readily trusted the proud strength, the favour of God. Then doffed he the iron coat of mail and his helmet from his head, and gave his sword bedecked, the choicest of weapons, to a thane that was serving, and bade him to hold ready his armour. Then the good man spoke some words of boasting: 'I reck not myself meaner in war-powers and works of battle than Grendel doth himself. For I will not with sword put him to sleep and be taking his life away, though well I might do it. He knows not of good things, that he may strike me, or hew my shield, though brave he may be in hostile working – but we two by right will forbear the sword if he dare be seeking warfare without weapon, and then God all-knowing, the holy Lord, shall adjudge the glory on whichever side He may think meet.' Then the bold in fight got him to rest, and the pillow received the head of the earl, and many a keen sea-warrior lay down on his bed in the hall about him. None of them thought that he thence would ever seek another dear home, folk or free city where he was a child; for they had heard that fell death had taken, ere this too many, in that wine-hall, of the people of the Danes. But the Lord gave weavings of war-speed to the people of the Geats, both comfort and help. So that they all overcame their enemies through the craft of one man and by his might only. And truly it is said that God Almighty doth wield for ever the race of men. Then came in the wan night the shadow-goer gliding. Warriors were sleeping when they should have been keeping guard over that palace; all save one only. It was well known to men that their constant foe could not draw them into shadowy places when the Creator was unwilling. But he, ever wakeful, in angry mood, and fiercely indignant against the foe, was waiting the issue.

ELEVEN

<u>THEN CAME GRENDEL,</u> stalking from the moors among the misty hill-slopes, and he bore God's anger. And the wicked scather of human kind fully intended to ensnare a certain one in the high hall. So he wended his way under the welkin to where he knew that the best of wine-halls, the gold-hall of man, was adorned with gold plating. Nor was that the first time that he sought out the home of Hrothgar. Nor ever in former or later days did he find a harder welcome from hall-thanes. Then the creature bereft of all joy came to the great hall, and the door, strongly bound with fire-bands, soon sprang open at his touch. And the evil-minded one in his fury burst open the door of the palace. And soon after this the enemy, angry in mind, was treading o'er the doomÈd floor. And a fearsome light streamed forth from his eyes likest to a flame. And he could see many a warrior in that palace, a troop of peace-lovers asleep together, a company of kinsmen, and he laughed aloud. Then the terrible monster fully intended to cut off from life every one of them there, when he was expecting abundance of meat. But that fate was not yet, that he should lay hold of any more of human kind after that night.

Then did Beowulf, kinsman of Hygelac, see the dire distress, how the wicked scather would fare with sudden grip. Nor did the monster think to delay, but at the first he quickly laid hold of a sleeping warrior, and tore him to pieces all unawares, and bit at the flesh and drank the streaming blood, and devoured huge pieces of flesh. And soon he had eaten up both feet and hands of the man he had killed. Then he stepped up to the great-hearted warrior[16] where he lay on the bed, and took him in his hands. He reached out his hand against the enemy, and quickly received him with hostile intent, and sat upon his arm. The Keeper of crimes soon was finding that he never had met in all the quarters of the earth amongst other men a greater hand-grip. And in mind and heart he was fearful, and eager to be gone and to flee away into darkness to seek the troop of devils. But that was not his fate, as it had been in days of yore. Then the good kinsman of Hygelac remembered the evening talk, and stood upright and laid hold upon him. His fingers burst. The giant

---

16   i.e. Beowulf.?

was going forth, but the earl stepped after. The famous one intended to escape more widely, howsoever he might, and to flee on his way thence to the sloping hollows of the fens. That journey was sorrowful, which the harmful scather took to Hart. The lordly hall resounded. And great terror there was to all the Danes, the castle-dwellers, to each of the brave. And both the mighty guardians were fiercely angry. The hall resounded. Then was it great wonder that the wine-hall withstood the bold fighters, and that it fell not to the earth, that fair earth-dwelling. But very firm it was standing, cunningly shaped by craft of the smith, within and without. Then on the floor was many a mead-bench, as I have heard tell, decked out with gold, where the fierce ones were striving. Nor did the wise Danes formerly suppose that any man could break down a hall so noble and decorated with antlers, or cunningly destroy it, unless the bosom of flame swallowed it up in smoke. The roaring went up now enough. And an awful terror came to the North Danes, to each one of those who heard weeping from the ramparts, the enemy of God singing a fierce song, a song that was empty of victory, and the captive of hell lamenting his sorrow. For he that was strongest of men in strength held him fast on the day of his life.

TWELVE

THE PRINCE OF EARLS would not at all let go alive the murderous comer, nor did he count his life as of use to any of the peoples. And many an earl of Beowulf's brandished the old heirloom, and were wishful to defend the life of their far-famed liege-lord, if they might do so. And they knew not, when they entered the battle, they the hard-thinking ones, the battle-men, and they thought to hew on all sides seeking out his spirit, that not any choice iron over the earth nor any battle weapon could be greeting the foe, but that he had forsworn all victorious weapons and swords. And miserable should be his passing on the day of this life, and the hostile sprite should journey far into the power of devils. Then he found out that, he who did crimes long before this with mirthful mind to human kind, he who was a foe to God, that his body would not last out; but the proud kinsman of Hygelac had him in his hands. And each was loathsome to the other while he lived. The terrible monster, sore with wounds was waiting. The gaping wound was seen on his shoulder. His sinews sprang open; and the bone-lockers burst. And great victory was given to Beowulf. Thence would Grendel, mortally wounded, flee under the fen-slopes to seek out a joyless dwelling. The more surely he knew he had reached the end of his life, the number of his days. Joy befell all the Danes after the slaughter-rush. So he had cleansed the hall of Hrothgar – he who had come from far, the proud and stout-hearted one, and saved them from strife. He rejoiced in the night-work and in the glorious deeds. His boast he had fulfilled, this leader of the Geats, which he made to the East Danes, and likewise made good all the distresses and the sorrows which they suffered of yore from the foe, and which through dire need they had to endure, of distresses not a few. And when the battle-brave man laid down the hand, the arm and shoulder under the wide roof, that was the manifest token.

THIRTEEN

THEN IN THE MORNING, as I have heard say, was many a battle-warrior round about the gift-hall. Came the folk-leaders from far and from near along the wide ways to look at the marvel. Nor did his passing seem a thing to grieve over to any of the warriors of those who were scanning the track of the glory-less wight, how weary in mind he had dragged along his life-steps, on the way thence doomed and put to flight, and overcome in the fight at the lake of the sea-monsters. There was the sea boiling with blood, the awful surge of waves all mingled with hot gore. The death-doomÈd one dyed the lake when void of joys he laid down his life in the fen for refuge. And hell received him. Thence after departed the old companions, likewise many a young one from the joyous journeys, proud from the lake to ride on mares, the youths on their horses. And there was the glory of Beowulf proclaimed. And many a one was saying that no man was a better man, no, none in the whole wide world under arch of the sky, of all the shield-bearers, neither south nor north, by the two seas. Nor a whit did they blame in the least their friend and lord, the glad Hrothgar; for he was a good king.

Meanwhile the famed in battle let the fallow mares leap and go faring forth to the contest, wherever the earth-ways seemed fair unto them and well known for their choiceness: and the thane of the king, he who was laden with many a vaunt, and was mindful of songs, and remembered a host of very many old sagas, he found other words, but bound by the truth. And a man began wisely to sing the journey of Beowulf, and to tell skilful tales with speeding that was good, and to interchange words. He told all that ever he had heard concerning Sigmund,[17] with his deeds of courage, and much that is unknown, the strife of Waelsing; and the wide journeys which the children of men knew not at all, the feud and the crimes, when Fitela was not with him, when he would be saying any of such things, the uncle to the nephew, for always they were comrades in need at all the strivings. They had laid low very many of the giant's race by means of the sword. And after his death-day a no little fame sprang up for Sigmund when he, the hard in battle,

17   Thus we see how sagas or legends came to be woven together into a song. See Appendix X.?

killed the worm, the guardian of the hoard. He alone the child of the Atheling, hazarded a fearful deed, under the grey stone. Nor was Fitela with him. Still it happened to him that his sword pierced through the wondrous worm, and it stood in the wall, that doughty iron, and the dragon was dead. And so this monster had gained strength in that going so that he might enjoy the hoard of rings by his own doom. He loaded the sea-boat and bore the bright treasures on to the ship's bosom, he the son of Waels. The worm melted hot. He was of wanderers the most widely famous in deeds of courage, amongst men, the protector of warriors. He formerly throve thus. Then the warfare of Heremod[18] was waning, his strength and his courage, and he was betrayed among the giants into the hands of the foes, and sent quickly away. And too long did whelming sorrow vex his soul. He was a source of care to his people, to all the nobles, and many a proud churl often was lamenting in former times the way of life of the stout-hearted, they who trusted him for the bettering of bales, that the child of their lord should always be prospering, and succeed to his father's kingdom, and hold the folk, the hoard and city of refuge, the kingdom of heroes, the country of the Danes. But Beowulf Hygelac's kinsman was fairer to all men; but crime assailed Heremod.[19]

Sometimes they passed along the fallow streets contending on mares. Then came the light of morning and hastened forth. And many a stiff-minded messenger went to the high hall to see the rare wonder. Likewise the King himself, the ward of the hoard of rings, came treading all glorious and with a great suite, forth from the bridal bower, and choice was his bearing, and his Queen with him passed along the way to the Mead-hall with a troop of maidens.

18   Heremod was a King of the Danes, and is introduced, says Wyatt, as a stock example of a bad King.?
19   Wyatt's translation.?

FOURTEEN

HROTHGAR SPAKE. He went to the hall and stood on the threshold and saw the steep roof all decked out with gold and the hand of Grendel. 'Let thanks be given quickly to God for this sight,' said he. 'Often I waited for the loathsome one, for the snares of Grendel. May God always work wonder after wonder, He the Guardian of glory. It was not long ago that I expected not a bettering of any woes for ever, when, doomed to blood, this best of all houses stood all stained with gore. Now has this Hero done a deed, through the power of the Lord, which none of us formerly could ever perform with all our wisdom. Lo! any woman who gave birth to such a son among human kind, may say, if she yet live, that the Creator was gracious unto her in bearing of children. Now, O Beowulf, I will love thee in heart as my son. Hold well to this new peace. Nor shall there be any lack of joys to thee in the world, over which I have power. Full oft I for less have meted out rewards and worshipful gifts to a meaner warrior, one weaker in strife. Thou hast framed for thyself mighty deeds, so that thy doom liveth always and for ever. May the All-wielder ever yield thee good as He now doth.'

Beowulf spake, the son of Ecgtheow: 'We framed to fight that brave work with much favour, and hazarded a deed of daring and the might of the unknown. I quickly gave you to see the monster himself the enemy in his fretted armour ready to fall. I thought to twist him quickly with hard grip on a bed of slaughter so that he should lie in the throes of death, because of my hand-grip, unless he should escape with his body. But I could not cut off his going when the Creator willed it not. I cleft him not readily, that deadly fiend. He was too strong on his feet. Nevertheless he left behind his hand as a life protection to show the track, his arm and his shoulders. But not by any means thus did that wretched creature get any help, nor by that did the evil-doer, brought low by sin, live any longer. But sorrow hath him in its fatal grip closely encompassed with baleful bands. There shall a man covered with sins be biding a mickle doom as the shining Creator will prescribe.'

Then was the man silent, the son of Ecglaf, in his boasting speech about deeds of battle, when the Athelings looked at the hand high up on the roof, by the craft of the earl, and the fingers of the foe, there before each one. And each of the places of the nails was likest to steel, the claw of the heathen, the uncanny claw of the battle warrior. Every one was saying that no very good iron, of any of the brave ones, would touch him at all, that would bear away thence the bloody battle-hand of the monster.

FIFTEEN

THEN WAS IT BIDDEN that Hart should be decked by their hands on the inside. And many there were of the men and wives who adorned that wine-hall the guest-chamber. And the tapestries shone along the walls brocaded with gold; many a wonderful sight for every man who stareth upon them. And that bright dwelling was greatly marred, though within it was fast bound with iron yet the door-hinges had sprung apart. The roof alone escaped all safe and sound when the monster turned to flight despairing of life and doomed for his crimes. Nor will it be easy to escape from that fate, whosoever may try to, but he shall get by strife the ready place of the children of men of the soul-bearers, who dwell upon earth, by a fate that cannot be escaped where his body shall sleep after the banquet fast in the tomb.

Then was the time for Healfdene's son to go into the hall, when the King himself would partake of the banquet. Nor have I ever heard tell that any people in greater numbers bore themselves better about their treasure-giver. And the wealthy ones sat down on the bench and rejoiced in their feeding. And full courteously their kinsmen took many a mead-cup, they the stout-hearted Hrothgar and Hrothulf in the high hall. And within was Hart filled with friends. And by no means were the Danes the while framing treacheries. Then the son of Healfdene gave to Beowulf the golden banner, the decorated staff banner as a reward for his conquest, and the helm and the byrny. And many a one saw the youth bear in front the bejewelled sword. Beowulf took the cup in the hall. Nor did he need to be ashamed of the fee-gift in the presence of warriors. Nor have I heard tell of many men giving to others on any ale-bench, four gifts gold-decked, in friendlier fashion. The outside rim wound with wires gave protection to the head on the outer side around the crown of the helmet. So that many an heirloom[20] could not hurt fiercely the helmet that was hardened by being plunged in cold water when the shield-warrior should attack the angry one. The Protector of earls commanded eight horses to be brought in under the barriers, with bridles gold plated. And a varicoloured saddle was fixed

---

20   Byrny was a coat of mail. Swords were of greater value as they were ancient heirlooms, and had done good service.?

upon one of them, decked out with treasures, and this was the battle-seat of the high King when the son of Healfdene would be doing the sword-play. Never in the van did it fail the warrior so widely kenned when the helmets were falling. Then the Prince of the Danes gave to Beowulf the wielding of them both, of horses and weapons; and bade him well enjoy them. And thus in manly fashion the famous chieftain, the treasure-guardian of heroes, rewarded the battle onslaught with horses and treasures so as no man can blame them, whoever will be saying rightly the truth.

SIXTEEN

THEN THE LORD OF earls as he sat on the mead-bench gave glorious gifts to each one of those who had fared with Beowulf over the ocean-ways, and heirlooms they were; and he bade them atone for that one with gold whom formerly Grendel had wickedly killed as he would have done more of them unless Almighty God and the spirit of Beowulf had withstood Weird. The Creator ruleth all of human kind, as still He is doing. And good understanding is always the best thing, and forethought of mind. And he who long enjoys here the world in these strife-days, shall be biding both pleasant and loathsome fate. Then was there clamour and singing together in the presence of the battle-prince of Healfdene, and the harp was sounded and a song often sung, when Hrothgar's scop would tell forth the hall-mirth as he sat on the mead-bench.

'When Fear was befalling the heirs of Finn,[21] the hero of the Half-Danes, and Hnaef of the Danes must fall in the slaughter of the Frisian People. Not in the least did Hildeburh need to be praising the troth of the Jutes. For sinlessly was she deprived of her dear ones in the play of swords of children and brothers. By fate they fell, wounded by arrows. And she was a sad woman. Nor without reason did the daughter of Hoc[22] mourn their doom. When morning light came, and she could see under the sky the murder of her kinsmen where she before in the world had the greatest of joy. For warfare took away all the thanes of Finn except a mere remnant, so that he could not in the place where they met fight any warfare at all with Hengest, nor seize from the Prince's thane the woful leavings by fighting. But they offered him terms, so that they all made other room for them on the floor, and gave them halls and a high seat that they might have half the power with the children of the Jutes; and the son of Folcwalda[23] honoured the Danes every day with fee-givings, and bestowed rings on the troop of Hengest, yea, even great treasures plated with gold, so that he would be making the kin of the Frisians bold in the beer-hall. Then they swore on both sides a treaty of peace. Finn swore with Hengest and all without strife that he

21   See Appendix VI.?
22   i.e. Hildeburh, wife of Finn.?
23   i.e. Finn.?

held in honour the woful remnant by the doom of the wise men, and that no man there by word or work should break the treaty, or ever annul it through treacherous cunning, though they followed the slayers of their Ring-giver, all bereft of their lord as was needful for them. But if any one of the Frisians by daring speech should bring to mind the murderous hate between them, then should the edge of the sword avenge it. Then sworn was that oath, and massive gold was lifted up from the hoard. Then was Hnaef, the best of the warriors, of the bold Danes, ready on the funeral pyre. And the blood-stained shirt of mail was easily seen, the golden boar, in the midst of the flame, the iron-hard boar,[24] and many an Atheling destroyed by wounds. Some fell on the field of death. Then Hildeburh commanded her very own son to be thrust in the flames of the pyre of Hnaef, his body to be burned and be put in the fire. And great was the moaning of the mother for her son, and dirge-like lamenting as the warrior ascended. And the greatest of slaughter-fires wound its way upwards towards the welkin and roared before the cavern. Heads were melting, wounds burst asunder. Then blood sprang forth from the wounds of the body. Flame swallowed all, that most cruel of ghosts, of both of those folk whom battle destroyed. Their life was shaken out.

---

24   The boar then, as ever since, occupied a prominent place in heraldry.?

SEVENTEEN

'THEN THE WARRIORS WENT forth to visit the dwellings which were be-reft of friends, and to look upon the land of the Frisians, the home-steads and the high town. And Hengest was still dwelling with Finn, that slaughter-stained winter, all bravely without strife. And he thought on the homeland, though he could not be sailing his ringed ship over the waters. The sea boiled with storm and waged war with the wind. And winter locked up the ice-bound waves till yet another year came in the court, as still it doth, which ever guards the seasons, and the glory-bright weather. Then winter was scattered, and fair was the bosom of the earth.[25] And the wanderer strove to go, the guest from the court. And much more he thought of vengeance for the feud than of the sea-voyage, as to how he could bring about an angry encounter, for he bore in mind the children of the Jutes. And so he escaped not the lot of mortals when Hunlafing did on his arm the best of swords, the flashing light of the battle, whose edge was well known to the Jutes. And dire sword-bale after befel the fierce-minded Finn, even in his very own home, when Guthlaf and Oslaf lamented the grim grip of war and the sorrow after sea-journeys, and were charging him with his share in the woes. Nor could he hold back in his own breast his fluttering soul. Then again was the hall adorned with the bodies of foemen, and Finn was also slain, the King with his troop, and the Queen was taken. And the warriors of the Danes carried to the ships all the belongings of the earth-king, such as they could find in the homestead of Finn, of ornaments and jewels. They bore away also the noble wife Hildeburh down to the sea away to the Danes, and led her to her people.'

So a song was sung, a lay of the gleemen, and much mirth there was and great noise from the benches. And cup-bearers offered wine from wondrous vessels. Then came forth Queen Wealtheow in her golden circlet, where the two good men were sitting, the uncle and his nephew. And still were they in peace together, and each true to the other. Likewise Unferth the Spokesman sat there at the foot of the Lord of the Danes. And each of them trusted Unferth's good heart

25   See a similar passage in my version of Sir Gawain and the Green Knight, Canto II. 1 and 2.?

and that he had a great soul, though he was not loyal to his kinsmen at the sword-play.

Then spake the Queen of the Danes: 'Take this cup, O my liege lord, thou giver of rings. Be thou right joyful, thou gold-friend to men; do thou speak mild words to the Geats, as a man should be doing. Be glad of thy Geats and mindful of gifts. Now thou hast peace both near and far. There is one who told me that thou wouldst have the battle-hero for thy son. Now Hart is all cleansed, the bright hall of rings. Enjoy whilst thou mayest many rewards, and leave to thy kinsmen both folk and a kingdom when thou shalt go forth to look on eternity. I know my glad Hrothulf[26] will hold in honour this youth if thou, O Hrothgar the friend of the Danes, dost leave the world earlier than he. I ween that he will yield good to our children if he remembers all that has passed – how we two worshipfully showed kindness to him in former days when he was but a child.' Then she turned to the bench where were her sons Hrothric and Hrothmund and the children of heroes, the youths all together. There sat the good man Beowulf of the Geats, by the two brothers.

26   Hrothulf, nephew of Hrothgar.?

EIGHTEEN

AND THE CUP WAS borne to them, and a friendly invitation given to them in words, and twisted gold was graciously proffered him, two arm-ornaments, armour and rings, and the greatest of neck-rings of which I heard tell anywhere on earth. Ne'er heard I of better hoard jewels of heroes under the sky, since Hama carried away the Brosinga-men[27] to the bright city, ornaments and treasure vessel. It was he who fled from the cunning plots of Eormanric[28] and chose eternal gain. Hygelac of the Geats next had the ring, he who was the grandson of Swerting, when under the standard he protected the treasure and defended the plunder. And Weird carried him off when he, because of pride suffered woes, the feud with the Frisians. Then carried he the jewels, the precious stones over the sea, he who was the ruling prince, and he fell under shield; and the life of the king and the coat of mail and ring together came into possession of the Franks. And worse warriors plundered the slaughter after the war. And the corpses of the Geats held the field of death. The hall resounded with noise when Wealtheow spake these words in the midst of the court:

'Enjoy this ring, dearest Beowulf, and use this coat of mail, these national treasures, and good luck befall thee! Declare thyself a good craftsman, and be to these boys gentle in teaching, and I will be mindful of thy guerdon for that thou hast so acted that men will esteem thee far and near for ever and ever, even as widely as the sea doth encompass the windy earth-walls. Be a noble Atheling as long as thou livest. I give thee many treasures. Be thou kindly in deed to my sons, joyful as thou art. For here is each earl true to his fellow, and mild of mood, and faithful to his liege-lord. Thanes are gentle, the people all ready. O ye warriors who have drunk deep, do as I tell you.' She went to the seat where was a choice banquet, and the men drank wine. They knew not Weird, the Fate that was grim, as it had befallen many an earl.

Then evening came on, and Hrothgar betook him to his own quarters, the Prince to his resting-place, and a great number of earls kept

27   See Appendix III.?
28   See Appendix IV.?

guard o'er the palace as often they had done in former days. They laid bare the bench-board and spread it over with beds and bolsters. And one of the beer-servants eager and fated went to his bed on the floor. And they set at his head war-shields, that were bright. And over the Atheling, there on the bench was easily seen the towering helmet and the ringed byrny, the glorious spear. It was their wont to be ready for war both at home and in battle, at whatever time their lord had need of them. The season was propitious.

NINETEEN

Then they sank down to sleep. And sorely some of them paid for their evening repose, as full often it had happened to them since Grendel came to the gold-hall and did evil, until an end was made of him, death after sins. It was easily seen and widely known to men that an avenger survived the loathsome one, for a long time after the war-sorrow. A woman, the mother of Grendel, a terrible wife, bore in mind her woes. She who was fated to dwell in the awful lake in the cold streams since Cain became a sword-slayer to his only brother, his father's son. He then went forth marked for the murder, and fled from human joys and dwelt in the waste. And thence he awoke many a fatal demon. And Grendel was one of them, the hateful fierce wolf, who found the man wide awake awaiting the battle. And there was the monster at grips with him, yet he remembered the main strength the wide and ample gift which God gave to him, and trusted in the favour of the Almighty for himself, for comfort and help by which he vanquished the enemy and overcame the hell-sprite. Then he departed abject, bereft of joy, to visit the death-place, he the enemy of mankind.

But his mother, greedy and sad in mind would be making a sorrowful journey that she might avenge the death of her son. She came then to Hart, where the Ring-Danes were asleep in that great hall. Then soon there came misfortune to the earls when the mother of Grendel entered the chamber. Yet less was the terror, even by so much as the craft of maidens, the war-terror of a wife,[29] is less than that of men beweaponed – when the sword hard bound and forged by the hammer, and stained with blood, cuts the boar on the helmet of the foe with its edge. Then in the hall, the hard edge was drawn, the sword over the seats, and many a broad shield, heaved up fast by the hand. And no one heeded the helmet nor the broad shield when terror seized upon them. She was in great haste, she would go thence her life to be saving when she was discovered. Quickly she had seized one of the Athelings fast in her grip when forth she was fleeing away to the fen-land. He was to Hrothgar the dearest of heroes, in the number of his comrades by the two seas, a powerful shield-warrior, whom she killed as he slumbered, a youth

29   Wyatt's translation.?

of renown. Beowulf was not there. To another the place was assigned after the treasure-gift had been bestowed on the famous Geat. Then a great tumult was made in Hart, and with bloodshed she had seized the well-known hand of Grendel her son. And care was renewed in all the dwellings. Nor was that a good exchange that they on both sides should be buying with the lives of their friends.

Then was the wise King, the hoar battle-warrior, rough in his mood when he came to know that the dearest of his chief thanes was dead and bereft of life. And Beowulf quickly was fetched into the bower, he, the man all victorious. And at the dawning went one of the earls, a noble champion, he and his comrades, where the proud man was waiting, to see whether the All-wielder will ever be causing a change after woe-spells. And the battle-worthy man went along the floor with his band of followers (the hall wood[30] was resounding) so that he greeted the wise man with words, the Lord of the Danes, and asked him if he had had a quiet night in spite of the pressing call.

30   That is, 'the harp'?

TWENTY

HROTHGAR SPAKE, he the Lord of the Danes: 'Ask not after our luck, for sorrow is renewed to the folk of the Danes. Aeschere is dead, the elder brother of Yrmenlaf; he was my councillor and my rune-teller,[31] my shoulder-companion when we in the battle protected our heads; when troops were clashing and helmets were crashing. He was what an earl ought to be, a very good Atheling. Such a man was Aeschere. And a wandering slaughter-guest was his hand-slayer, in Hart. I know not whither that dire woman exulting in carrion, and by her feeding made famous, went on her journeys. She was wreaking vengeance for the feud of thy making when thou killedst Grendel but yesternight, in a violent way, with hard grips, because all too long he was lessening and destroying my people. He fell in the struggle, gave his life as a forfeit; and now comes another, a mighty man-scather, to avenge her son, and the feud hath renewed as may seem a heavy heart-woe to many a thane who weeps in his mind over the treasure-giver. Now lieth low the hand which availed you well, for every kind of pleasure. I heard land-dwellers, and hall-counsellors, and my people, say that they saw two such monstrous March-steppers,[32] alien-sprites, holding the moorland. And one of them was in the likeness of a woman as far as they could tell; the other, shapen wretchedly, trod the path of exiles in the form of a man, except that he was greater than any other man, he whom in former days the earth-dwellers called by name Grendel. They knew not his father, whether any secret sprite was formerly born of him. They kept guard over the hidden land, and the wolf-slopes, the windy nesses, the terrible fen-path where the mountain streams rush down under mists of the nesses, the floods under the earth. And it is not farther hence than the space of a mile where standeth the lake, over which are hanging the frosted trees, their wood fast by the roots, and shadowing the water. And there every night one may see dread wonders, fire on the flood. And there liveth not a wise man of the children of men who knoweth well the ground. Nevertheless the heath-stepper, the strong-horned hart, when pressed by the hounds

31   Rune – literally, 'a secret'.?
32   Cp. the phrase 'Welsh marches', i.e. the boundaries or limits of Wales.?

seeketh that woodland, when put to flight from afar, ere on the hill-side, hiding his head he gives up his life.[33]

'Nor is that a canny place. For thence the surge of waters riseth up wan to the welkin when stirred by the winds, the loathsome weather, until the heaven darkens and skies weep. Now is good counsel depending on thee alone. Thou knowest not the land, the terrible places where thou couldest find the sinful man; seek it if thou darest. I will reward thee for the feud with old world treasures so I did before, with twisted gold, if thou comest thence, on thy way.'

---

33   Cp. description of hunting in Sir Gawain and the Green Knight, Canto III. 2.?

BEOWULF SPAKE, the son of Ecgtheow: 'Sorrow not, O wise man. It is better for each one to avenge his friend, when he is much mourning. Each one of us must wait for the end of his world-life. Let him work who may, ere the doom of death come; that is afterwards best for the noble dead. Arise, O ward of the kingdom. Let us go forth quickly to trace out the going of Grendel's kinswoman. I bid thee do it. For neither in the bosom of the earth, nor in forests of the mountains, nor by the ways of the sea, go where she will, shall she escape into safety. Do thou this day be patient in every kind of trouble as I also hope to be.' The old man leapt up and gave thanks to God, the mighty Lord, for the words of Beowulf.

Then was bridled a horse for Hrothgar, a steed with twisted hair, and as a wise prince he went forth in splendid array. The troop of shield-warriors marched along. And the traces were widely seen in the forest-ways, the goings of Grendel's mother over the ground. Forwards she had gone over the mirky moorlands, and had borne in her grasp, bereft of his soul, the best of the thanes who were wont to keep watch over Hrothgar's homestead. Then Beowulf, the Atheling's child, stepped o'er the steep and stony slopes and the narrow pathways, and the strait-ened single tracks, an unknown way, by the steep nesses, and by many a sea-monster's cavern. And one of the wise men went on before to seek out the path, until all at once he found some mountain trees, over-hanging the grey stones, a forest all joyless. And underneath was a wa-ter all bloodstained and troubled. And a grievous thing it was for all the Danes to endure, for the friends of the Scyldings,[34] and for many a thane, and distressful to all the earls, when they came upon the head of Aeschere on the cliffs above the sea. The flood boiled with blood and with hot gore (the folk looked upon it). And at times the horn sounded a battle-song ready prepared.

All the troop sat down. And many kinds of serpents they saw in the water, and wonderful dragons searching the sea, and on the cliff-slopes, monsters of the ocean were lying at full length, who at the morning tide often make a woful journey on the sail-path; and snakes

---

34   Scyldings are the Danes.?

and wild beasts they could see also. And these living things fell down on the path all bitter and angry when they perceived the noise, and the blast of the war-horn. And the Prince of the Geats killed one of them with his bow and arrows and ended his wave-strife, and he was in the sea, slower at swimming as death swept him away. And on the waves by fierce battle hard pressed, and with boar-spears savagely barbed, the wondrous sea-monster was assailed in the struggle and drawn up on the headland. And men were looking at the awful stranger. And Beowulf put on him his armour, that was fitting for an earl, and by no means did he lament over his life, for the hand-woven coat of mail, which was ample and of many colours, was destined to explore the deeps, and knew well how to defend his body, so that neither battle-grip nor the hostile grasp of the treacherous one might scathe breast or life; and the white helmet thereof warded his head, that which was destined to search out the bottom of the sea and the welter of waters, and which was adorned with treasures and encircled with noble chains, wondrously decked and set round with boar-images, as in days of yore a weapon-smith had made it for him, so that no brand nor battle-sword could bite him. And by no means was that the least of aids in battle that the Spokesman of Hrothgar[35] lent him at need, even the hilted sword which was called Hrunting. And it was one of the ancient treasures. Its edge was of iron, and poison-tipped, and hardened in battle-sweat. And never did it fail in the fight any man who brandished it in his hands, or who dared to go on fearful journeys, to the field of battle. And that was not the first time that it was to do deeds of courage. And Unferth did not think, he the kinsman of Ecglaf, crafty of strength, of what he formerly had said[36] when drunken with wine, he had lent that weapon to a braver sword-warrior. He himself durst not risk his life in the stress of the waters and do a glorious deed. And thereby he lost his doom of famous deeds. But thus was it not with that other, for he had got himself ready for the battle.

35   i.e. Unferth.?
36   Cp. Chapter VIII.?

TWENTY TWO

BEOWULF SPAKE, the son of Ecgtheow: 'O kinsman of Healfdene,[37] thou far-famed and proud prince, thou gold-friend of men, now that eager I am for this forth-faring, bethink thee now of what we two were speaking together, that if I should lose my life through helping thee in thy need, thou wouldst be always to me in the place of a father after my death. Be thou a guardian to my kinsmen, my thanes, and my hand comrades, if battle should take me. And dear Hrothgar, send thou the gifts, which thou didst give me, to Hygelac. And the Lord of the Geats, the son of Hrethel, when he looks on the treasure and perceives the gold, will see that I found a giver of rings, one good and open-handed, and that while I could, I enjoyed the treasures. And do thou let Unferth, the man who is far-famed, have the old heirloom, the curiously wrought sword with its wave-like device, with its hard edge. I work out my fate with Hrunting, or death shall seize me.'

After these words the Lord of the Weder-Geats courageously hastened, and by no means would he wait for an answer. The whelming sea received the battle-hero. And it was a day's while before he could see the bottom of the sea. And very soon the fierce and eager one who had ruled the expanse of the floods for a hundred years, she, the grim and greedy, saw that a man was searching out from above the dwelling of strange monsters. Then she made a grab at him, and closed on the warrior with dire embrace. But not at first did she scathe his body, safe and sound. The ring surrounded it on the outside, so that she could not pierce the coat of mail or the interlaced war-shirt with loathsome finger. Then the sea-wolf, when she came to the bottom of the sea, bore the Ring-Prince towards her house so that he might not, though he was so strong in soul, wield any weapon; and many a wonder oppressed him in the depths, many a sea-beast broke his war-shirt with his battle-tusks, and monsters pursued him.

Then the earl saw that he was in he knew not what hall of strife, where no water scathed him a whit, nor could the sudden grip of the flood touch him because of the roof-hall. He saw, too, a firelight, a bright pale flame shining. Then the good man caught sight of the she-

37   i.e. Hrothgar.?

wolf, that monstrous wife, down in the depths of the sea. And he made a mighty rush with his sword. Nor did his hand fail to swing it so that the ringed mail on her head sang a greedy death-song. Then Beowulf the stranger discovered that the battle-blade would not bite or scathe her life, but the edge failed the lord in his need. It had suffered many hand-blows, and the helmet, the battle-dress of the doomed one, it had often cut in two. That was the first time that his dear sword-treasure failed him. Then he became resolute, and not by any means did he fail in courage, that kinsman of Hygelac, mindful of glory. And this angry warrior threw away the stout sword, bound round with jewels with its wavy decorations, and with its edge of steel, so that it lay prone on the ground; and henceforth he trusted in his strength and the hand-grasp of might. So should a man be doing when he thinketh to be gaining long-lasting praise in fighting, and careth not for his life. Then the Lord of the Geats seized by the shoulder the mother of Grendel (nor at all did he mourn over that feud), and he, the hard in battle, threw down his deadly foe, when he was angry, so that she lay prone on the floor. But she very quickly, with grimmest of grips, requited him a hand-reward, and made a clutch at him. And the weary in soul, that strongest of fighters, he the foot-warrior stumbled and fell. Then she sat on that hall-guest, and drew forth her axe, broad and brown-edged, and would fain be avenging the death of her child, of her only son. But on his shoulder was the coat of mail all woven, which saved his life and prevented the entrance of the point and the edge of the sword. And the son of Ecgtheow, the Prince of Geats, would have surely gone a journey under the wide earth unless that warlike coat of mail had given him help, that hard war-net, and unless the Holy God He the cunning Lord, and the Ruler in the heavens, had wielded the victory, and easily decided the issue aright; then he straightway stood up.

TWENTY THREE

THEN AMONG THE WEAPONS he caught sight of a sword, rich in victories, an old weapon of the giants, and doughty of edge, the glory of warriors. It was the choicest of weapons, and it was greater than any other man could carry to the battle-playing, and all glorious and good, a work of the giants. And he seized it by the belted hilt, he the warrior of the Danes, rough and battle-grim, and he brandished the ring-sword; and despairing of life, he angrily struck so that hardly he grasped at her neck and broke the bone-rings. And the point pierced through the doomed flesh-covering. And she fell on the floor. The sword was all bloody, and the man rejoiced in his work. Shone forth the bright flame and a light stood within, even as shineth the candle[38] from the bright heavens. And then he looked on the hall, and turned to the wall. And the thane of Hygelac, angry and resolute, heaved hard the weapon, taking it by the hilt. And the edge was not worthless to the battle-warrior, for he would be quickly requiting Grendel many a war-rush which he had done upon the West Danes, many times oftener than once when in sleeping he smote the hearth-comrade of Hrothgar, and fed on them sleeping, of the Danish folk, some fifteen men, and bore forth yet another one, that loathly prey. And well he requited him, this furious champion, when he saw the war-weary Grendel lying in death, all void of his life as formerly in Hart the battle had scathed him. His body sprang apart when after his death he suffered a stroke, a hard battle-swing; and then he struck off his head.

Right soon the proud warriors, they who with Hrothgar, looked forth on the sea, could easily see, that the surging water was all stained with blood and the grey-haired ancients spoke together about the good man, that they deemed not the Atheling would ever again come seeking the famous Prince Hrothgar glorying in victory, for it seemed unto many that the sea-wolf had destroyed him.

Then came noonday. The valiant Danes left the headland, and the gold-friend of men[39] went homeward thence. And the strangers of the Geats, sick in mind, sat and stared at the water. They knew and expected

---

38   i.e. the sun.?
39   Hrothgar.?

not that they would see again their liege-lord himself. Then the sword began to grow less, after the battle-sweat, into icicles of steel. And a wonder it was that it all began tŏ melt likest to ice, when Our Father doth loosen the band of frost and unwinds the icicles, He who hath power over the seasons, He is the true God. Nor in these dwellings did the Lord of the Geats take any other treasure, though much he saw there, except the head and the hilt, decked out with jewels. The sword had melted, and the decorated weapon was burnt up. The blood was too hot, and so poisonous the alien sprite who died in that conflict. Soon Beowulf was swimming, he who formerly awaited the onset of the hostile ones in the striving, and he dived upwards through the water. And the weltering surge and the spacious lands were all cleansed when the alien sprite gave up his life and this fleeting existence.

He the stout-hearted came swimming to shore, he the Prince of the sea-men enjoying the sea-spoils, the great burden of that which he had with him. They advanced towards him and gave thanks to God, that glorious crowd of thanes, and rejoiced in their lord that they could see him once more. Then was loosed quickly from that valiant man both helmet and shield. The sea became turbid, the water under welkin, all stained with blood. And rejoicing in spirit the brave men went forth with foot-tracks and passed over the earth, the well-known pathways. And a hard task it was for each one of those proud men to bear that head away from the sea-cliff. Four of them with difficulty on a pole were bearing the head of Grendel to the gold-hall, until suddenly, valiant and battle-brave, they came to the palace, fourteen of the Geats marching along with their liege-lord who trod the field where the mead-hall stood. Then this Prince of the thanes, this man so bold of deed and honoured by Fate, this battle-dear warrior went into the hall to greet King Hrothgar. Then over the floor where warriors were drinking they bore Grendel's head, a terror to the earls and also to the Queen. And men were looking at the splendid sight of the treasures.

TWENTY FOUR

BEOWULF SPAKE, the son of Ecgtheow: 'Lo, son of Healfdene, lord of the Danes, we have brought thee this booty of the sea all joyfully, this which thou seest as a token of glory. And I hardly escaped with my life, and hazarded an arduous task of war under water. And nearly was the battle ended for me, but that God shielded me. Nor could I in that conflict do aught with Hrunting, though the weapon was doughty. But the Ruler of men granted me to see hanging on the wall a beauteous sword mighty and ancient (often He guides those who are bereft of their comrades), and I drew the weapon. And I struck in that striving the guardian of the house when I saw my chance. Then that battle-sword that was all decked out, burned up so that blood gushed forth, the hottest of battle-sweat. But I bore off that hilt thence from the enemy, and wrought vengeance for the crimes, the deaths of the Danes, as it was fitting. And here I bid thee to take thy rest all sorrowless in Hart, with the troop of thy men and each of the thanes of thy people, the youth and the doughty ones. O Lord of the Danes, no longer need'st thou fear for them, because of earls' life-bale as before thou didst.' Then was the golden hilt, the work of the giants, given into the hand of the old warrior, the hoary battle-chief. This work of the wonder-smiths went into the possession of the Lord of the Danes after the destruction of devils; and when the man of the fierce heart, the adversary of God guilty of murder, forsook this world, it passed to the best of world-kings by the two seas, of these who in Sceden Isle dealt out treasures.

Hrothgar spake and looked upon the hilt, the old heirloom on which was written the beginning of the ancient feud since the flood, the all-embracing ocean slew the giant race, when they bore themselves pre-sumptuously. They were a folk strangers to the eternal God, to whom the ruler gave their deserts through whelming of waters. Thus was there truly marked on the sword guards of shining gold, by means of rune-staves, set down and stated by whom that sword was wrought at the first, that choicest of weapons, with its twisted hilt, adorned with a dragon. Then spake the wise man the son of Healfdene, and all kept silence: 'He who doeth truth and right among the folk, and he who can recall the far-off days, he the old protector of his country may say that this earl was well born. Thy fair fame is spread throughout the wide ways, among all peoples, O my friend Beowulf. Thou dost hold all with patience, and might, with the proud of mind. I will perform the compact as we two agreed. Thou shalt be a lasting aid to thy people, a help to the heroes. Not so was Heremod[40] to the sons of Egwela, the honour-full Danish folk.[41] For he did not become a joy to them, but slaughter and death to the Danish people. But in a fury he killed the table-companions his boon comrades; until he alone, the famous chieftain, turned away from human joys. And though the mighty God greatly exalted him by the joys of strength over all people and rendered him help, yet a fierce hoard of hate grew up in his soul; no rings did he give to the Danes, as the custom was; and joyless he waited, so that he suffered troublesome striving and to his people a long time was baleful. Do thou be learning by that example and seek out manly virtues. I who am old in winters sing thee this song. And a wonder is it to say how the mighty God giveth wisdom to mankind through wideness of mind, lands, and earlship. He hath power over all. Sometimes he letteth the thought of man of famous kith and kin be turning to love, and giveth him earth-joys in his own country, so that he holdeth the city of refuge among men, and giveth him to rule over parts of the world, and very wide kingdoms, so that he himself foolishly never thinketh of his end. He dwelleth in weal; and neither disease nor old age doth deceive him a whit, nor doth hostile sorrow darken his mind, nor anywhere do strife or sword-hate show themselves; but all the world doth go as he willeth.

---

40   Cp. pp. 66–68.?
41   'Honour-full' is Wyatt's translation.?

TWENTY FIVE

'He knoweth no evil until his share of pride wasteth and groweth, while sleepeth the guardian, the ward of his soul. And the sleep is too deep, bound up in afflictions, and the banesman draweth near who shooteth cruelly his arrows from the bow. Then in his soul under helmet is he stricken with bitter shaft. Nor can he save himself from the crooked behests of the cursed ghost. And little doth he think of that which long he hath ruled. And the enemy doth covet, nor at all doth he give in boast the plated rings, and he then forgetteth and despiseth his fate his share of honour which God before gave him, He the Wielder of wonder. And in the end it doth happen that the body sinks fleeting and doomed to death falleth. And another succeeds thereto who joyfully distributeth gifts, the old treasure of the earl, and careth not for terrors. Guard thee against malicious hate, O my dear Beowulf, thou noblest of men, and choose for thyself that better part, eternal wisdom. Have no care for pride, O glorious champion. Now is the fame of thy strength proclaimed for a while. Soon will it be that disease or sword-edge or grasp of fire or whelming of floods or grip of sword or flight of arrow or dire old age will sever thee from strength, or the lustre of thine eyes will fail or grow dim. Then forthwith will happen that death will o'erpower thee, O thou noble man. Thus have I for fifty years held sway over the Ring-Danes under the welkin and made safe by war many a tribe throughout the world with spears and swords, so that I recked not any man my foeman under the sweep of heaven. Lo! then there came to me change in my homeland, sorrow after gaming, when Grendel, that ancient foe became my invader. And ever I bore much sorrow of mind through that feud. And may God be thanked, the eternal lord, that I lingered in life, till I looked with mine eyes on that head stained with sword-blood after the old strife. Go now to thy seat and enjoy the feasting, thou who art glorious in war. And when morning cometh there shall be a host of treasures in common between us.'

And the Geat was glad of mind, and soon he went up to the high seat as the proud chief had bidden him. Then renewed was fair chanting as before 'mongst these brave ones who sat on the floor. And the helmet of night grew dark over men. And the noble warriors arose. The venerable king wished to go to his bed, the old prince of the Danes. And the Geat, the shield-warrior, desired greatly to go to his rest. And straightway a hall-thane guided the far-comer, weary of his journey, he who so carefully attended to all his needs such as that day the ocean-goers would fain be having. And the great-hearted one rested himself. The House towered on high that was spacious and gold-decked. The guest slept within until the black raven heralded the joy of heaven.

Then came the sun, hastening and shining over the earth. Warriors were hurrying and Athelings were eager to go to their people. The bold-hearted comer would visit the ship far away. He the hardy one bade the son of Ecglaf carry forth Hrunting, and commanded him to take his sword, that lovely piece of steel. And he gave thanks for the lending, and said he reckoned him a good war-comrade and crafty in fighting. Not at all did he blame the edge of the sword. He was a proud man. When ready for the journey were all the warriors, then Beowulf the Atheling, of good worth to the Danes, went up to the dais where was Hrothgar the faithful and bold, and greeted him there.

TWENTY SIX

BEOWULF SPAKE, the son of Ecgtheow: 'Now we the sea-farers, that have come from afar, desire to say that we are hastening back to Hygelac. And here have we been nobly waited on, and well thou hast treated us. And if I then on earth can gain a whit further greater heart-love from thee, O Lord of men, than I have gained already, in doing war-deeds, thereto I'm right ready. And if I shall hear o'er the sheet of waters that terrors are oppressing those who sit round thee, as erewhile thine enemies were doing upon thee, I will bring here a thousand thanes, heroes to help thee. And I know that Hygelac, the Lord of the Geats, the guardian of my folk, though young in years, will help me by word and works to bring to thee honour and bear spear to thine aid, the help of strength, if thou hast need of men. And if Hrethric[42] the Prince's child should ever take service in the court of the Geat, he may find there many a friend. It is better for him who is doughty himself to be seeking far countries.'

Hrothgar spake and gave him answer: 'The all-knowing Lord doth send thee words into thy mind. Never heard I a man speak more wisely, so young in years, thou art strong of main and proud of soul, and of words a wise sayer. I reckon that if it cometh to pass that an arrow or fierce battle should take away the children of Hrethel or disease or sword destroy thy sovereign, the protector of the folk, and thou art still living, that the Sea-Geats will not have to choose any better king, if thou wilt hold the kingdom of the kinsmen. Thou hast brought about peace to the folk of the Geats and the Spear-Danes, and a ceasing of the strife and of the enmity which formerly they suffered. And whilst I am ruling the wide kingdom, treasures shall be in common between us. And many a man shall greet another with gifts over the sea.[43] And the ring-necked ship shall bear over the ocean both offerings and love-tokens. I know the two peoples to be steadfast towards friend and foe, and blameless in all things in the old wise.'

Then in that hall the prince of the earls, the son of Healfdene, gave him twelve treasures, and bade him be seeking his own people in safe-

---

42   Hrethric, one of Hrothgar's sons.?
43   Literally, 'the gannet's bath.' The sea is also 'Swan's path,' 'Sail-path,' &c.?

ty and with the offerings, and quickly to come back again. Then the King, the Prince of the Danes, he of good lineage, kissed the best of thanes, and embraced his neck. And tears were falling down the face of the old man. And the old and wise man had hope of both things, but most of all of the other that they might see each the other, those thoughtful men in council.

For Beowulf was so dear to him that he could not restrain the whelming in his bosom, but a secret longing fast in the bonds of his soul was burning in his breast against his blood.[44] So Beowulf the warrior, proud of his golden gifts, went forth o'er the grassy plain rejoicing in treasure. And the sea-goer was awaiting her lord where she lay at anchor. And as he was going he often thought on the gift of Hrothgar. He was a king, blameless in every way, until old age, that scather of many, bereft him of the joys of strength.

---

44   A difficult phrase. Refers perhaps to old feuds between Danes and Geats.?

TWENTY SEVEN

So MANY A PROUD young warrior came to the seaside. And they were carrying the ring-net, the interlaced coats of mail. And the ward of the shore noticed the going of the earls, as he did their coming.[45] Nor with evil intent did he hail the guests from the edge of the cliff, but rode up to them, and said that welcome and bright-coated warriors went to the ship to the people of the Geats. Then on the sand was the spacious craft laden with battle-weeds, the ringed prow with horses and treasures, and the mast towered high over Hrothgar's gifts. And he gave to the captain a sword bound with gold, so that by the mead-bench he was by that the worthier because of the treasure and the heirloom. Then he went on board, the deep water to be troubling, and finally left the land of the Danes. And by the mast was one of the ocean-garments, a sail fast by a rope. The sea-wood thundered. Nor did the wind hinder the journey of that ship. The ocean-goer bounded forth, the foamy-necked one, over the waves, the bound prow over the ocean streams, till they could see the cliffs of the Geats' land, the well-known headlands.

Then the keel thronged up the shore, driven by the wind, and stood fast in the sand. And the harbour-master was soon on the seashore, who of yore eagerly had seen from afar the going forth of the dear men. And he made fast the wide-bosomed ship, by the anchor chains, so that the less the force of the waves could tear away that winsome ship. He commanded the treasure of the nobles to be borne up the beach, the fretted armour and the plated gold. And not far thence it was for them to be seeking the giver of treasure, Hygelac, Hrethel's son, for at home he dwelleth, he and his companions near to the sea-wall. And splendid was that building, and the Prince was a bold King, and the halls were high, and Hygd his wife was very young and wise and mature in her figure, though the daughter of HÆreth had bided in that city but a very few years. But she was not mean nor niggardly of gifts and of treasures to the people of the Geats.

---

45   Cp. Chapter III.?

But Thrytho[46] was fierce, for she had committed a terrible crime, that bold Queen of the folk. There was none that durst risk that dire thing of the dear companions, save only her lord, that he should stare on her with his eyes by day; but if he did he might expect that death-bands were destined for himself, for after the hand-grip a weapon was quickly prepared, that the sword that was curiously inlaid should bring to light and make known the death-bale. Nor is it a queenly custom for a woman to perform, though she might be peerless, that she should assail the life of a peace-wearer, of her dear lord, after a pretended insult. At least King Offa, the kinsman of Hemming, checked her in that. But otherwise said the ale-drinkers, namely that she did less of bale to her people and of hostile acts, since the time when she was first given all decked with gold to the young champion,[47] to her dear lord, since she sought the Hall of Offa over the fallow flood by the guidance of her father, where on the throne whilst she lived she well did enjoy her fate, that woman famous for good works. And she kept great love for the prince of heroes, and of all mankind he was, as I have learned by asking, the greatest by two seas. For Offa was a spear-keen man in gifts and in warfare, and widely was he honoured. And he ruled his people wisely. And to him and Thrytho EomÆr was born to the help of heroes, he the kinsman of Hemming, the nephew of Garmund, was crafty in battle.

---

46   Thrytho is referred to as a foil to Hygd. Thrytho was as bad a woman as Hygd was good. She was a woman of a wild and passionate disposition. She became the Queen of King Offa, and it seems to have been a case of the 'taming of the shrew.' Offa appears to have been her second husband. See below.?

47   i.e. to Offa.?

TWENTY EIGHT

THEN THE HARDY ONE himself, with his troop set forth to tread the seashore, going along the sands, the wide sea-beaches. The candle of the world shone, the sun that was shining from the South. And joyfully they journeyed, and with courage they marched along, to where they heard by inquiring, that the good Prince of earls, the banesman of Ongentheow[48] the young war-king, was giving out rings within the city. And quickly was made known to Hygelac the coming of Beowulf, that he the Prince of warriors, the comrade in arms, was returning alive and hale from the battle-play, was coming to the palace. And straightway was there room made for the foot-guests on the floor of the hall by command of the King. And he that had escaped scot-free from the contest sat with the King, kinsman with kinsman, and the lord with courteous speech saluted the brave man with high-swelling words. And the daughter of HÆreth[49] poured forth from the mead-cups throughout that great hall, for she loved well the people, and carried round the drinking-stoups to each of the warriors. And Hygelac began to question his comrade as curiosity prompted him as to the journey of the Sea-Geats. 'How went it with thee, dear Beowulf, in thy faring, when thou didst bethink thee suddenly to be seeking a contest o'er the salt waters, in battle at Hart? And thou didst requite the widely known woe which Hrothgar was suffering, that famous lord. And I brooded o'er that mind-care with sorrow-whelmings, for I trusted not in the journey of the dear man. And for a long time I bade thee not a whit to be greeting the murderous stranger, but to let the South Danes themselves wage war against Grendel. And I now give God thanks that I see thee safe and sound.'

Beowulf answered, the son of Ecgtheow: 'O Lord Hygelac, it is well known to many a man, our famous meeting, and the battle we fought, Grendel and I, on the wide plain, when he was working great sorrow to the Danes and misery for ever. All that I avenged, so that no kinsman of Grendel anywhere on earth needed to boast of that uproar by twilight, no not he of that kindred who liveth the longest, encircled

---

48   i.e. Hygelac; see Appendices VII. and IX.?
49   i.e. Hygd, Queen of the Geats, Hygelac's wife.?

by the fen. And first, to greet Hrothgar, I went to the Ring-hall. And straightway the famous kinsman of Healfdene, when he knew my intention, gave me a place with his own son; and the troop was all joyful. Nor ever have I seen greater joy amongst any hall-dwellers under the arch of heaven. Sometimes the famous Queen,[50] the peace-bringer of the folk, walked over the whole floor and encouraged the young sons. And often she gave to the man a twisted ring ere she went to the high seat. And sometimes for the noble band the daughter of Hrothgar carried the ale-cups to the earls at the end of the high table. And I heard those who sat in that hall calling her Freawaru as she gave the studded treasure to the heroes. And she, young and gold-decked, is betrothed to the glad son of Froda.[51] The friend of the Danes and the guardian of the kingdom has brought this to pass, and taken that counsel, so as to set at rest by that betrothal many a slaughter-feud and ancient strife. And often it happens that a little while after the fall of a people, the deadly spear seldom lieth at rest though the bride be doughty. And this may displease the lord of the Heathobards and all of his thanes of the people, when he with his bride walketh over the floor, that his doughty warriors should attend on a noble scion of the Danes, and the heirloom of the ancients should glisten on him, all hard, and the ring-sword, the treasure of the Heathobards, whilst they might be wielding weapons.[52]

50   i.e. Wealtheow, Hrothgar's Queen.?
51   i.e. Ingeld. See below.?
52   Another episode, viz. that of Freawaru and Ingeld. Note also the artificial break of the narrative into chapters. See Appendix V.
Hrothgar's hopes by the marriage of his daughter Freawaru to Ingeld of the Heathobards was doomed to disappointment, cp. 'Widsith,' 45–9.?

TWENTY NINE[53]

'TILL THE DAY ON which they risked their own and their comrades' lives in the battle. Then said an old spear-warrior who remembered all that had happened, the death of men by spears (his mind was grim), and he began with sorrowful mind to seek out the thought of the young champion by broodings of the heart, and to awaken the war-bales, and this is what he said: "Canst thou recognize, my friend, the dire sword which thy father carried to the battle, under the visored helm, on that last journey, when the Danes slew him and had the battle-field in their power, when Withergyld[54] lay dead after the fall of the heroes? Now here the son of I know not which of the slayers, all boasting of treasures, goeth into the hall and boasteth of murder and carrieth the gift which thou shouldst rightly possess." Then he exhorteth and bringeth to mind each of the occasions with sorrowful words, until the time cometh that the thane of the bride dieth all stained with blood for the deeds of his father by the piercing of the sword, having forfeited his life. But the other thence escapeth alive, for he knows the land well. Then the oath-swearing of earls is broken on both sides when deadly enmities surge up against Ingeld, and his love for his wife grows cooler after whelming care. And for this reason I reckon not sincere the friendliness of the Heathobards towards the Danes or the troop-peace between them, the plighted troth.

'Now I speak out again about Grendel, for that thou knowest full well, O giver of treasure, how went that hand-to-hand fight of the heroes. When the jewel of heaven glided over the world, then the angry sprite, the terrible and evening-fierce foe, came to visit us where we were dwelling in the hall all safe and sound. There was battle impending to Hondscio, the life-bale to the doomed one. And he first fell, the champion begirt. For Grendel was to the famous thane a banesman by biting, and devoured whole the dear man. Nor would he, the bloody-toothed slayer, mindful of bales, go out empty-handed any sooner again, forth from the gold-hall; but he proved my strength of main, and ready-handed he grasped at me. An ample and wondrous glove hung fast by cun-

53   Numbers XXIX. and XXX. are lacking in the MS. The divisions here are as in Wyatt's edition.?
54   Withergyld – name of a Heathobard warrior.?

ning bands. And it was cunningly fashioned by the craft of devils, and with skins of the dragon. And the fierce doer of deeds was wishful to put me therein, one among many. But he could not do so, for I angrily stood upright. And too long would it be to tell how I requited all evil to that scather of the people, where I, O my liege-lord, honoured thy people by means of good deeds. He escaped on the way, and for a little while he enjoyed life-pleasures. But his right hand showed his tracks in Hart, and he sank to the bottom of the sea, all abject and sad of heart. And the lord of the Danes rewarded me for that battle-rush with many a piece of plated gold, and with ample treasure, when morning came and we had set ourselves down to the feasting. And there was singing and rejoicing. And the wise man of the Danes, who had learned many things, told us of olden days. And the bold in battle sometimes touched the harp-strings, the wood that was full of music, and sometimes he gave forth a song that was true and sad – and sometimes, large-hearted, the King related a wondrous spell well and truly.[55] And sometimes the old man encumbered by years, some ancient warrior, lamented his lost youth and strength in battle. His heart was tumultuous when he, of many winters, recalled all the number of them. So we rejoiced the livelong day until another night came down upon men. Then was the mother of Grendel quickly ready for vengeance, and came on a woful journey, for Death had carried off her son, that war-hate of the Geats. And the uncanny wife avenged her child. And Aeschere, that wise and ancient councillor, departed this life. Nor when morning came might the Danish people burn him with brand, that death-weary man, nor lay the beloved man on the funeral pyre. For she bore away the body in her fiendish grip under the mountain-streams. And that was to Hrothgar the bitterest of griefs which for long had befallen the Prince of the people. Then the Prince, sad in mood, by thy life entreated me that I should do a deed, worthy of an earl, midst welter of waters, and risk my life and achieve glory. And he promised me rewards. I then discovered the grim and terrible guardian of the whelming waters, at the sea's bottom, so widely talked of. There was a hand-to-hand engagement between us for a while, and the sea boiled with gore; I cut off the head of Grendel's mother in the hall at the bottom of the sea, with powerful sword. And I scarce saved my life in that conflict. But not yet was my doomsday. And afterwards the Prince of earls gave me many gifts, he the son of Healfdene.

---

55   Probably referring to the chanting of some ancient legend by the scop, or gleeman.?

THIRTY

Missing in the original text.

THIRTY ONE

'So in good customs lived the King of the people. Nor had I lost the rewards, the meed of strength, for the son of Healfdene bestowed upon me treasures according to my choice, which I will bring to thee, O my warrior-King, and graciously will I proffer them. Again all favour depends on thee, for few chief kinsmen have I save thee, O Hygelac.' He commanded them to bring in the boar, the head-sign, the battle-steep helmet, the hoary byrny, the splendid war-sword, and then he chanted this song: 'It was Hrothgar, that proud prince, who bestowed upon me all this battle-gear. And a certain word he uttered to me, that I should first give thee his kindly greeting.[56] He said that Hrothgar the King of the Danes possessed it a long while. Nor formerly would he be giving the breast-weeds to his son the brave Heoroward, though dear he was to him. Do thou enjoy all well.'

Then I heard that four horses, of reddish yellow hue, followed the armour. And thus he did him honour with horses and gifts. So should a kinsman do. By no means should they weave cunning nets for each other, or with secret craft devise death to a comrade. His nephew was very gracious to Hygelac, the brave in strife, and each was striving to bestow favours on the other. And I heard that he gave to Hygd the neck-ring so curiously and wondrously wrought, which Wealtheow a daughter of royal birth had given him, and three horses also slender and saddle-bright. And her breast was adorned with the ring she had received.

And Beowulf, son of Ecgtheow, so famous in warfare and in good deeds, bore himself boldly and fulfilled his fate, nor did he slay the drunken hearth-comrades. He was not sad-minded, but he, the battle-dear one, by the greatest of craft known to man held fast the lasting and generous gift which God gave him. For long had he been despised, so that the warriors of the Geats looked not upon him as a good man, nor did the lord of troops esteem him as of much worth on the mead-bench. Besides, they thought him slack and by no means a warlike Atheling. Then came a change from all his distresses to this glorious man. Then the Prince of Earls, the battle-brave King, commanded that the heirloom of Hrethel all decked out in gold should be

56   Wyatt's translation.?

brought in. For of swords there was no more glorious treasure among the Geats. And he laid it on the bosom of Beowulf, and gave him seven thousand men and a building and a throne. And both of them held the land, the earth, the rights in the land as an hereditary possession; but the other who was the better man had more especially a wide kingdom.

And in after-days it happened that there were battle-crashings, and Hygelac lay dead,[57] and swords under shields became a death-bane to Heardred,[58] when the brave battle-wolves, the Swedes, sought him out among the victorious ones and assailed with strife the nephew of Hereric, and it was then that the broad kingdom came into the possession of Beowulf. And he held sway therein fifty winters (and a wise King was he, that old guardian of his country) until on dark nights a dragon began to make raids, he that watched over the hoard in the lofty cavern, the steep rocky cave. And the path thereto lay under the cliffs unknown to men. And what man it was who went therein I know not, but he took from the heathen hoard a hall-bowl decked with treasure. Nor did he give it back again, though he had beguiled the guardian of the hoard when he was sleeping, by the craft of a thief. And Beowulf found out that the dragon was angry.[59]

---

57   Hygelac was killed in his historical invasion of the Netherlands, which is five times referred to in the poem. See Appendix VII.?

58   See Appendix IX.?

59   The MS. here is very imperfect. I have used the emended text of Bugge, which makes good sense. See Appendix XII.?

THIRTY TWO

AND IT WAS BY NO means of his own accord or self-will that he sought out the craft of the hoard of the dragon who inflicted such evil upon himself, but rather because being compelled by miseries, the slave fled the hateful blows of heroes, he that was shelterless and the man troubled by guilt penetrated therein. And soon it came to pass that an awful terror arose upon the guest.[60]... And in the earth-house were all kinds of ancient treasures, such as I know not what man of great thoughts had hidden there in days of old, the immense heirlooms of some noble race, costly treasures. And in former times death had taken them all away, and he alone of the warriors of the people who longest lingered there, full lonely and sad for loss of friends was he, and he hoped for a tarrying, that he but for a little while might enjoy the ancient treasures. And this hill was quite near to the ocean-waves, and to the sea-nesses, and no one could come near thereto.

And he the guardian of rings carried inside the cave the heavy treasures of plated gold, and uttered some few words: 'Do thou, O earth, hold fast the treasures of earls which heroes may not hold. What! From thee in days of yore good men obtained it. Deadly warfare and terrible life-bale carried away all the men of my people of those who gave up life. They had seen hall-joy. And they saw the joys of heaven. I have not any one who can carry a sword or polish the gold-plated cup, the dear drinking-flagon. The doughty ones have hastened elsewhere. The hard helmet dight with gold shall be deprived of gold plate. The polishers sleep the sleep of death who should make ready the battle grim, likewise the coat of mail which endured in the battle was shattered over shields by the bite of the iron spears and perishes after the death of the warrior. Nor can the ringed byrny go far and wide on behalf of heroes, after the passing of the war-chief.

'No joy of harping is there, nor mirth of stringed instruments, nor does the goodly hawk swing through the hall, nor doth the swift horse paw in the courtyard. And death-bale hath sent away many generations of men.' Thus then, sad at heart he lamented his sorrowful plight, one for many, and unblithely he wept both day and night

---

60   Here again the text is imperfect.?

until the whelming waters of death touched his heart. And the ancient twilight scather found the joyous treasure standing open and unprotected, he it was who flaming seeks the cliff-sides, he, the naked and hateful dragon who flieth by night wrapt about with fire. And the dwellers upon earth greatly fear him. And he should be seeking the hoard upon earth where old in winters he guardeth the heathen gold. Nor aught is he the better thereby.

And thus the scather of the people, the mighty monster, had in his power the hall of the hoard three hundred years upon the earth until a man in anger kindled his fury. For he carried off to his liege-lord the plated drinking-flagon and offered his master a treaty of peace. Thus was the hoard discovered, the hoard of rings plundered. And a boon was granted to the miserable man. And the Lord saw for the first time this ancient work of men. Then awoke the dragon, and the strife was renewed. He sniffed at the stone, and the stout-hearted saw the foot-mark of his foe. He had stepped too far forth with cunning craft near the head of the dragon. So may any one who is undoomed easily escape woes and exile who rejoices in the favour of the Wielder of the world. The guardian of the hoard, along the ground, was eagerly seeking, and the man would be finding who had deprived him of his treasure while he was sleeping. Hotly and fiercely he went around all on the outside of the barrow – but no man was there in the waste. Still he gloried in the strife and the battle working. Sometimes he returned to the cavern and sought the treasure vessels. And soon he found that one of the men had searched out the gold, the high heap of treasures. The guardian of the hoard was sorrowfully waiting until evening should come. And very furious was the keeper of that barrow, and the loathsome one would fain be requiting the robbery of that dear drinking-stoup with fire and flame. Then, as the dragon wished, day was departing. Not any longer would he wait within walls, but went forth girt with baleful fire. And terrible was this beginning to the people in that country, and sorrowful would be the ending to their Lord, the giver of treasure.

THIRTY THREE

THEN THE FIEND BEGAN to belch forth fire, and to burn up the glorious palace. And the flames thereof were a horror to men. Nor would the loathly air-flier leave aught living thereabouts. And this warfare of the dragon was seen far and wide by men, this striving of the foe who caused dire distress, and how the war-scather hated and harmed the people of the Geats. And he hurried back to his hoard and the dark cave-hall of which he was lord, ere it was day-dawn. He had encircled the dwellers in that land with fire and brand. He trusted in his cavern, and in battle and his cliff-wall. But his hope deceived him. Then was the terror made known to Beowulf, quickly and soothly, namely that his very homestead, that best of houses, that throne of the Geats, was dissolving in the whelming fire. And full rueful was it to the good man, and the very greatest of sorrows.

And the wise man was thinking that he had bitterly angered the Wielder of all things, the eternal God, in the matter of some ancient customs.[61] And within his breast gloomy brooding was welling, as was by no means his wont. The fiery dragon had destroyed by flame the stronghold of the people, both the sea-board and neighbouring land. And therefore the King of the Weder-Geats devised revenge upon him.

Now Beowulf the Prince of earls and protector of warriors commanded them to fashion him a glorious war-shield all made of iron. For he well knew that a wooden shield would be unavailing against flames. For he, the age-long noble Atheling, must await the end of days that were fleeting of this world-life, he and the dragon together, though long he had held sway over the hoard of treasure. And the Prince of rings scorned to employ a troop against the wide-flying monster in the great warfare. Nor did he dread the striving, nor did he think much of this battle with the dragon, of his might and courage, for that formerly in close conflict had he escaped many a time from the crashings of battle since he, the victorious sword-man, cleansed the great hall in Hart, of Hrothgar his kinsman, and had grappled in the contest with the mother of Grendel, of the loathly kin.

---

61   Possibly a later insertion, 'the ten commandments' (Wyatt).?

Nor was that the least hand-to-hand fight, when Hygelac was slain there in the Frisian land when the King of the Geats, the friendly lord of the folk, the son of Hrethel, died in the battle-rush beaten down by the sword, drunk with blood-drinking. Then fled Beowulf by his very own craft and swam through the seas.[62] And he had on his arm alone thirty battle-trappings when he went down to the sea. Nor did the Hetware need to be boasting, of that battle on foot, they who bore their linden shields against him. And few of them ever reached their homes safe from that wolf of the battle.

But Beowulf, son of Ecgtheow, swam o'er the expanse of waters, miserable and solitary, back to his people, where Hygd proffered him treasures and a kingdom, rings and dominion. She did not think that her son Heardred would know how to hold their native seats against strangers, now that Hygelac was dead. Nor could the wretched people prevail upon the Atheling (Beowulf) in any wise to show himself lord of Heardred or to be choosing the kingship. Nevertheless he gave friendly counsel to the folk with grace and honour until that he (Heardred) was older and held sway over the Weder-Geats.

Then those exiles the sons of Ohthere sought him over the seas; they had rebelled against the Lord of the Swedes, the best of the sea-kings, that famous chieftain of those who bestowed rings in Sweden. And that was life's limit to him. For the son of Hygelac, famishing there, was allotted a deadly wound by the swing of a sword. And the son of Ongentheow went away thence to visit his homestead when Heardred lay dead, and left Beowulf to sit on the throne and to rule the Goths. And he was a good King.[63]

---

62   Beowulf saved his life by swimming across the sea, in Hygelac's famous raid. See Appendix VII.?

63   See Appendix IX.?

THIRTY FOUR

HE WAS MINDED IN after-days to be requiting the fall of the prince. He was a friend to the wretched Eadgils, and helped Eadgils the son of Ohthere with an army with warriors and with weapons, over the wide seas. And then he wrought vengeance with cold and painful journeyings and deprived the king (Onela) of life.[64] Thus the son of Ecgtheow had escaped all the malice and the hurtful contests and the courageous encounters, until the day on which he was to wage war with the dragon. And so it came to pass that the Lord of the Geats went forth with twelve others and inflamed with fury, to spy out the dragon. For he had heard tell of the malice and hatred he had shown to men, whence arose that feud.

And by the hand of the informer,[65] famous treasure came into their possession; he was the thirteenth man in the troop who set on foot the beginning of the conflict. And the sorrowful captive must show the way thither. He against his will went to the earth-hall, for he alone knew the barrow under the ground near to the sea-surge, where it was seething, the cavern that was full of ornaments and filagree. And the uncanny guardian thereof, the panting war-wolf, held possession of the treasures, and an ancient was he under the earth. And it was no easy bargain to be gaining for any living man.

So the battle-hardened King sat down on the cliff, and took leave of his hearth-comrades, he the gold-friend of the Geats. And his heart was sad, wavering, and ready for death, and Weird came very near to him who would be greeting the venerable warrior and be seeking his soul-treasure, to divide asunder his life from his body. And not long after that was the soul of the Atheling imprisoned in the flesh. Beowulf spake, the son of Ecgtheow: 'Many a war-rush I escaped from in my youth, in times of conflict. And well I call it all to mind. I was seven years old when the Lord of Treasures, the friendly lord of the folk, took me away from my father – and King Hrethel had me in thrall, and gave me treasure and feasted me and kept the peace. Nor was I a whit less dear a child to him than any of his own kin, Herebald and HÆthcyn or

64   See Appendix IX.?
65   See p. 138.?

my own dear Hygelac. And for the eldest was a murder-bed most un-happily made up by the deeds of a kinsman,[66] when HÆthcyn his lordly friend brought him low with an arrow from out of his horn-bow, and missing the mark he shot through his brother with a bloody javelin. And that was a fight not to be atoned for by gifts of money; and a crime it was, and wearying to the soul in his breast. Nevertheless the Atheling must unavenged be losing his life. For so is it a sorrowful thing for a venerable man to see his son riding the gallows-tree when he singeth a dirge a sorrowful song, as his son hangeth, a joy to the ravens. And he, very old, may not give him any help. And every morning at the feasting he is reminded of his son's journey else-whither. And he careth not to await another heir within the cities, when he alone through the fatality of death hath found out the deeds.

'Heartbroken he looks on the bower of his son, on the wasted wine-hall, become the hiding-place for the winds and bereft of the revels. The riders are sleeping, the heroes in the tomb. Nor is any sound of harping, or games in the courts as erewhile there were.

66   See Appendix VIII.?

THIRTY FIVE

'THEN HE GOETH TO the sleeping-place and chanteth a sorrow-song, the one for the other. And all too spacious seemed to him the fields and the dwelling-house. So the Prince of the Geats bore welling heart-sorrow after Herebald's death, nor a whit could he requite the feud on the murderer, nor visit his hate on that warrior with loathly deeds, though by no means was he dear to him. He then forsook the joys of life because of that sorrow-wound which befell him, and chose the light of God, and left to his sons land and towns when he departed this life as a rich man doth. Then was there strife and struggle between the Swedes and the Geats, and over the wide seas there was warfare between them, a hardy battle-striving when Hrethel met with his death. And the children of Ongentheow were brave and battle-fierce, and would not keep the peace on the high seas, but round about Hreosnaborg they often worked terrible and dire distress. And my kinsmen wrought vengeance for that feud and crime as all men know, though the other bought his life with a hard bargain. And war was threatening HÆthcyn the lord of the Geats. Then I heard tell that on the morrow one brother the other avenged on the slayer with the edge of the sword, whereas Ongentheow[67] seeketh out Eofor. The warhelmet was shattered, and the Ancient of the Swedes fell prone, all swordpale. And well enough the hand kept in mind the feud and withheld not the deadly blow. And I yielded him back in the warfare the treasures he gave me with the flashing sword, as was granted to me. And he gave me land and a dwelling and a pleasant country. And he had no need to seek among the Gifthas or the Spear-Danes or in Sweden a worse war-wolf, or to buy one that was worthy.

'And I would always be before him in the troop, alone in the front of the battle, and so for ever will I be striving, whilst this sword endureth, that earlier and later has often stood me in good stead, since the days when for doughtiness I was a hand-slayer to Day Raven the champion of the Hugs. Nor was he fated to bring ornaments or breast-trappings to the Frisian King, but he the guardian of the standard, he the Atheling, fell on the battle-field, all too quickly. Nor was the sword-edge his bane, but the battle-grip broke the whelmings of his heart and the bones of

67   See Appendices VII. and IX.?

his body. Now shall my sword-edge, my hand and hard weapon, be fighting for the hoard.'

Beowulf moreover now for the last time spake these boastful words: 'In many a war I risked my life in the days of my youth, yet still will I seek a feud, I the old guardian of the people will work a glorious deed if the wicked scather cometh out from his earth-palace to seek me.'

Then he saluted for the last time each of the warriors, the brave wearers of helmets, the dear companions. 'I would not carry a sword or weapon against the dragon if I knew how else I might maintain my boast against the monster, as I formerly did against Grendel. But in this conflict I expect the hot battle-fire, both breath and poison. Therefore I have both shield and byrny. I will not flee from the warder of the barrow a foot's-space, but it shall be with me at the wall of the barrow as Weird shall direct, who created all men. I am strong in soul so that I will refrain from boasting against the war-flier. Await ye on the barrow guarded by byrnies, O ye warriors in armour, and see which of us two will better survive his wounds after the battle-rush. This is no journey for you nor fitting for any man save only for me, that he should share a conflict with the monster and do deeds worthy of an earl. I will gain possession of the gold by my courage, or battle and deadly evil shall take away your lord.'

Then the strong warrior, hard under helm, arose beside his shield and carried his shirt of mail under the rocky cliffs and trusted in the strength of himself alone. Nor was that a coward's journey. Then Beowulf, possessed of manly virtues, who had escaped in many a conflict and crashing of battle when men encountered on foot, saw standing by the wall of the barrow an arch of rock, and a stream broke out thence from the barrow, and the whelming of that river was hot with battle-fires. Nor could he survive any while near to the hoard unburnt because of the flame of the dragon. Then in a fury the Prince of the Weder-Geats let a torrent of words escape from his breast and the stout-hearted one stormed. And his war-clear voice resounded under the hoar cliffs. And hatred was stirred, for the guardian of the hoard recognized well the voice of Beowulf. And that was no time to be seeking friendship. And the breath of the monster, the hot battle-sweat, came forth from the rock at the first and the earth resounded. The warrior, the Lord of the Geats, raised his shield under the barrow against the terrible sprite. Now the heart of the dragon was stirred up to seek the conflict. The good war-king had formerly drawn his sword, the ancient heirloom, not slow of edge. And each of them who intended evil was a terror the one to the other. And the stern-minded one, he the Prince of friendly rulers, stood by his steep shield, and he and the dragon fell quickly together. Beowulf waited warily all in his war-gear. Then the flaming monster bent as he charged, hastening to his doom. The shield well protected life and body of the famous warrior for a lesser while than he had willed it if he was to be wielding victory in that contest on the first day; but Weird had not so fated it. And the Lord of the Geats uplifted his hand, and struck at the horribly bright one heavy with heirlooms, so that the edge stained with blood gave way on the bone and bit in less strongly than its master had need of when pressed by the business. Then after the battle-swing the guardian of the barrow was rough-minded and cast forth slaughter-fire. Battle-flames flashed far and wide. And the son of the Geats could not boast of victory in the conflict. The sword had failed him, naked in the battle, as was unfitting for so well tempered a steel. And it was not easy for the famous son of Ecgtheow to give up possession of the bottom of the sea, and that he should against his will dwell in some place far otherwise, as must each man let go these fleeting days sooner or later. And not long after this Beowulf and the monster met together again. The guardian of the hoard took good heart, and smoke was fuming in his breast. And fierce were his sufferings as the flames embraced him, he who before had ruled over the folk. Nor at all in a troop did his hand-comrades stand round him, that warrior of Athelings, showing courage in the battle, but they fled into a wood their lives to be saving. And the mind of one of them was surging with sorrows, for to him whose thoughts are pure, friendship cannot ever change.

THIRTY SIX

WIGLAF WAS HE CALLED, he who was the son of Weohstan, the beloved shield-warrior, the Prince of the Danes and the kinsman of Aelfhere. He saw his lord suffering burning pain under his visor. Then he called to mind the favour that he (Beowulf) had bestowed upon him in days of yore, the costly dwelling of the Waegmundings[68] and all the folk-rights which his father had possessed. Then he could not restrain himself, but gripped the shield with his hand, the yellow wood, and drew forth the old sword which was known among men as the heirloom of Eanmund, the son of Ohthere, and in the striving Weohstan was banesman by the edge of the sword to that friendless exile and bore away to his kinsman the brown-hued helmet, the ringed byrny, and the old giant's sword that Onela[69] had given him, the war-weeds of his comrade, and the well-wrought armour for fighting. Nor did he speak of the feud, though he slew his brother's son. And he held possession of the treasures many years, both the sword and the byrny, until such time as his son should hold the earlship as his father had done. And he gave to the Geats a countless number of each kind of war-weeds, when he in old age passed away from this life, on the outward journey. That was the first time for the young champion that he went into the war-rush with his noble lord. Nor did his mind melt within him, nor did the heirloom of his kinsman at the war-tide. And the dragon discovered it when they two came together.

Wiglaf spake many fitting words, and said to his comrades (for his mind was sad within him): 'I remember the time when we partook of the mead, and promised our liege-lord in the beer-hall, he who gave to us rings, that we would yield to him war-trappings both helmets and a hand-sword, if such need befell him. And he chose us for this warfare, and for this journey, of his own free will, and reminded us of glory; and to me he gave these gifts when he counted us good spear-warriors and brave helmet-bearers, although our lord, this guardian of the people had it in his mind all alone to do this brave work for us, for he most of all men could do glorious things and desperate deeds of war. And now is the

---

68   Waegmundings – the family to which both Beowulf and Wiglaf belonged.?
69   See Appendix IX.?

day come that our lord hath need of our prowess and of goodly warriors. Let us then go to the help of our battle-lord while it lasts, the grim terror of fire. God knows well of me that I would much rather that the flame should embrace my body together with that of my lord the giver of gold. Nor does it seem to me to be fitting that we should carry shields back to the homestead except we have first laid low the foe and protected the life of the Prince of the Weders.[70] And well I know that his old deserts were not that he alone of the youth of the Geats should suffer grief and sink in the fighting. So both sword and helmet, byrny and shield shall be common to both of us together.'

Then he waded through the slaughter-reek, and bore the war-helmet to the help of his lord, and uttered a few words: 'Beloved Beowulf, do thou be doing all things, as thou of yore in the days of thy youth wast saying that thou wouldst not allow thy glory to be dimmed whilst thou wast living. Now shalt thou, the brave in deeds and the resolute noble, save thy life with all thy might. I am come to help thee.' After these words came the angry dragon, the terrible and hostile sprite yet once again, and decked in his various hues of whelmings of fire, against his enemies, the men that he hated. And the wood of the shield was burnt up with the waves of flame, and his byrny could not help the young spear-warrior; yet did the youth bravely advance under the shield of his kinsman when his own had been destroyed by the flames. Then again the war-king bethought him of glory, and struck a mighty blow with his battle-sword so that it fixed itself in his head, forced in by violence. And Naegling, Beowulf's sword old and grey, broke in pieces, and failed in the contest. It was not given to him that sharp edges of swords should help him in battle. His hand was too strong, so that it overtaxed every sword, as I have been told, by the force of its swing, whenever he carried into battle a wondrous hand-weapon. And he was nowise the better for a sword. Then for the third time, the scather of the people, the terrible Fire-dragon, was mindful of feuds, and he rushed on the brave man when he saw that he had room, all hot and battle-grim, and surrounded his neck with bitter bones. And he was all be-bloodied over with life-blood, and the sweat welled up in waves.

70   i.e. Beowulf.?

THIRTY SEVEN

THEN I HEARD TELL that the Earl of the King of the People showed in his time of need unfailing courage in helping him with craft and keenness, as was fitting for him to do. He paid no heed to the head of the dragon (but the brave man's hand was being burnt when he helped his kinsman), but that warrior in arms struck at the hostile sprite somewhat lower in his body so that his shining and gold-plated sword sank into his body, and the fire proceeding therefrom began to abate. Then the good King Beowulf got possession of his wits again, and drew his bitter and battle-sharp short sword that he bore on his shield. And the King of the Geats cut asunder the dragon in the midst of his body. And the fiend fell prone; courage had driven out his life, and they two together had killed him, noble comrades in arms. And thus should a man who is a thane always be helping his lord at his need. And that was the very last victory achieved by that Prince during his life-work.

Then the wound which the Earth-dragon had formerly dealt him began to burn and to swell. And he soon discovered that the baleful venom was seething in his breast, the internal poison. Then the young noble looked on the giant's work as he sat on a seat musing by the cliff wall, how arches of rock, firmly on columns held the eternal earth-house within. Then the most noble thane refreshed his blood-stained and famous Lord, his dear and friendly Prince with water, with his own hands, and loosened the helmet for the battle-sated warrior. And Beowulf spake, over his deathly pitiful wound, for well he knew that he had enjoyed the day's while of his earthly joy: and the number of his days was all departed and death was coming very near.

'Now,' said Beowulf, 'I would have given battle-weeds to my son if any heir had been given to me of my body. I held sway over these peoples fifty years. And there was no folk-king of those who sat round about who dared to greet me with swords, or oppress with terror. At home have I bided my appointed time, and well I held my own[71], nor did I seek out cunning feuds, nor did I swear many unrighteous oaths. And I, sick of my life-wounds, can have joy of all this. For the

71   Wyatt and Morris's translations.?

Wielder of men cannot reproach me with murder of kinsmen when my life shall pass forth from my body. Now do thou, beloved Wiglaf, go quickly and look on the hoard under the hoar stone, now that the dragon lieth prone and asleep sorely wounded and bereft of his treasure. And do thou make good speed that I may look upon the ancient gold treasures and yarely be feasting mine eyes upon the bright and cunning jewels, so that thereby after gazing on that wealth of treasure I may the more easily give up my life and my lordship over the people, whom I have ruled so long.'

THIRTY EIGHT

THEN STRAIGHTWAY I heard tell how the son of Weohstan, after these words had been spoken, obeyed the behest of his lord, who was sick of his wounds, and carried the ring-net and the coat of mail adorned, under the roof of the barrow. And as Wiglaf, exulting in victory, came by the seat, he saw many gems shining and shaped like the sun[72] and gleaming gold all lying on the ground, and wondrous decorations on the wall, and he saw too the den of the dragon, the ancient twilight-flier, and flagons standing there and vessels of men of days long gone by, no longer polished but shorn of adornment. And there also was many a helmet, ancient and rusty, and many arm-rings cunningly twisted.

The possession of treasure and of gold on the earth may easily make proud all of mankind, let him hide it who will. Likewise he saw the all-gilded banner lying high over the hoard, that greatest of wondrous handiwork and all woven by the skill of human hands. And therefrom went forth a ray of light, so that he could see the floor of the cave, and look carefully at the jewels. And there was no sign of the dragon, for the sword-edge had carried him off.

Then I heard tell how in that barrow one at his own doom[73] plundered the hoard, that old work of giants, and bore away on his arms both cups and dishes. And the banner also he took, that brightest of beacons. Beowulf's sword, with its iron edge, had formerly injured him who had been the protector of these treasures for a long time, and had waged fierce flame-terror, because of the hoard fiercely welling in the midnight hour until he was killed.

The messenger[74] was in haste, and eager for the return journey, and laden with jewels, and curiosity tormented him as to whether he would find the bold-minded Prince of the Geats alive on the battle-field, and bereft of strength where before he had left him. Then he with the treasures found the glorious lord, his own dear master, at the last gasp, and all stained with blood. And he began to throw water upon him, until the power of speech brake through his mind, and Beowulf spake, and with sorrow he looked upon the hoard.

---

72   Wyatt and Morris translate 'sun jewels.'?
73   Wyatt's translation.?
74   i.e. Wiglaf.?

'I would utter words of thanks to the Lord and wondrous King, to the eternal God, for the treasures which now I am looking upon that I have managed to obtain them for my dear people before my death-day. Now that I have in exchange for this hoard of treasure sold my life in my old age, and laid it down, do thou still be helping the people in their need, for I may no longer be lingering here. Do thou bid the famous warriors erect a burial-mound, after the burning of the funeral pyre, at the edge of the sea, which shall tower aloft on Whale's Ness, as a memorial for my people, and so the sea-farers shall call it the Hill of Beowulf, even those who drive the high ships from afar through the mists of the flood.'

Then he the bold Prince doffed from his neck the golden ring. And he gave it to his thane, to the young spear-warrior, the gold-adorned helmet, the ring, and the byrny, and bade him enjoy it well. 'Thou, O Wiglaf,' he said, 'art the last heir of our race, of that of the Waegmundings. Weird has swept away all my kinsmen to their fated doom, all the earls in their strength, and I shall follow after them.'

Now that was the very last word of the old warrior's breast thoughts, ere he chose the funeral pyre the hot wave-whelmings. And his soul went forth from his breast to be seeking the doom of the truth-fast ones.

THIRTY NINE

THEN HAD IT SORROWFULLY come to pass for the young warrior that he saw his most beloved in a miserable plight on the earth at his life's end. Likewise the terrible dragon, his slayer, lay there bereft of life and pressed sore by ruin. And the coiled dragon could no longer wield the hoard of rings, but the iron edges of the sword, well tempered and battle-gashed; the hammer's leavings[75], had carried him off, so that the wide-flier, stilled because of his wounds, fell to the earth near to the hoard-hall. And no more in playful wise at the midnight hour, did he drift through the air; this dragon, proud in his gainings of treasure, showed not his face, but was fallen to the earth because of the handiwork of the battle-warrior.

And as I have heard, it would have profited but few of the mighty men, even though they were doughty in deeds of all kinds, though they should rush forth against the flaming breath of the poisonous scather, even to the very disturbing of the Ring-Hall with their hands, if they should have found the guardian thereof awake, and dwelling in the cliff-cave. Then Beowulf's share of lordly treasure was paid for by his death. And both he and the dragon had come to an end of their fleeting days.

And not long after that, the laggards in battle, those cowardly treaty-breakers, ten of them together, came back from the woodlands, they who erewhile had dreaded the play of javelins when their lord had sore need of their help. But they were filled with shame, and carried their shields, and battle-weeds, to where the old prince was lying. And they looked on Wiglaf; he the foot-warrior sat aweary near to the shoulders of his lord, and sought to rouse him by sprinkling water upon him, but he succeeded not at all. Nor could he, though he wished it ever so much, keep life in the chieftain or avert a whit the will of the Wielder of all things. Every man's fate was decided by the act of God, as is still the case. Then was a grim answer easily given by the young man to these who erewhile had lost their courage.

Wiglaf spake, he the son of Weohstan, the sad-hearted. 'He who will speak truth may say that the lord and master who gave you gifts, and warlike trappings, in which ye are now standing, when he very often

---

75   i.e. it had been well hammered into shape.?

gave on the ale-bench to them who sat in the hall, both helmet and byrny, the Prince to his thanes, as he could find any of you most noble far or near, that he wholly wrongly bestowed upon you war-trappings when war befell him. The King of the folk needed not indeed to boast of his army comrades, yet God, the Wielder of Victory, granted to him that alone he avenged himself with the edge of the sword when he had need of strength. And but a little life-protection could I give him in the battle, yet I sought to help him beyond my strength. The dragon was by so much the weaker when I struck with my sword that deadly foe. And less fiercely the fire surged forth from his head. Too few were the defenders thronged around their lord when his fated hour came. And now shall the receiving of treasure, and the gift of swords, and all joy of home and hope cease for ever to men of your kin. And every man of you of the tribe must wander empty of land-rights, since noble men will learn far and wide of your flight and inglorious deed. Death would be better for earls than a life of reproach.'

FOURTY

THEN HE BADE THEM announce that battle-work at the entrenchment up over the sea-cliff where that troop of earls sat sorrowful in soul through the morning-long day, holding their shields and in expectation of the end of the day and the return of the dear man. And he who rode to and fro o'er the headland was little sparing of fresh tidings, but said to all who were sitting there, 'Now is the joy-giver of the people of the Geats fast on his death-bed, and by the deed of the dragon he inhabits the place of rest gained by a violent death. And by his side lieth the enemy of his life, sick of his dagger-wounds. Nor could he inflict with the sword any wound on that monster. Wiglaf sits over Beowulf, he the son of Weohstan, the earl over the other one who is dead, and reverently keeps ward over the loathÈd and the belovÈd. But there is an expectation of a time of war to the people, since to Franks and Frisians the fall of the King has become widely known. The hard strife was shapen against the Hugs, when Hygelac came with a fleet into the Frisian lands[76] where the Hetware overcame him in battle, and by their great strength and courage brought it to pass that the shield-warrior should stoop. He fell in the troop. Nor did the Prince give jewelled armour to the doughty ones. The mercy of the Merewing[77] was not always shown to us. Nor do I expect aught of peace or good faith from the Swedish People. But it was well known that Ongentheow[78] bereft HÆthcyn the son of Hrethel[79] of life over against Ravenswood, when because of pride the warlike Swedes first sought out the people of the Geats. Soon Ongentheow the wise father of Ohthere, the ancient and terrible, gave him (HÆthcyn) a return blow, destroyed the sea-kings, and rescued his bride (Queen Elan) he the old man rescued his wife bereft of gold, the mother of Onela and of Ohthere, and then followed up the deadly foe until with difficulty they retreated all lord-less to Ravenswood. And he attacked the remnant[80] with a great army, weary though he

76   Yet another reference to Hygelac's famous raid. See Appendix VII.?
77   Merovingian King of the Franks.?
78   See Appendix IX.?
79   Hrethel, King of Geats, father of Hygelac and grandfather of Beowulf.?
80   Literally, 'the sword-leavings.'?

was with his wounds. And the live-long night he vowed woe upon the wretched troop, and said that on the morrow he would by the edge of the sword slay some and hang them up on the gallows-tree for a sport of the birds. But help came to the sorrowful in soul at the dawn of day, when they heard the horn of Hygelac and the blast of his trumpet when the good man came on the track faring with the doughty warriors of the people.

FOURTY ONE

'And the blood-track of both Swedes and Geats, the slaughter-rush of warriors, was widely seen how the folk stirred up the feud amongst them. The good man, wise and very sad, went away with his comrades to seek out a stronghold. Earl Ongentheow turned away to higher ground, for he the war-crafty one had heard of the prowess of Hygelac the proud. He had no trust in his power to resist, or that he would be able to refuse the demands of the seamen, the ocean-farers, or defend the treasure he had taken, the children and the bride.[81] Thence afterwards, being old, he sought refuge under the earth-wall. Then was chase given to the people of the Swedes and the banner of Hygelac borne aloft; and they swept o'er the field of peace when the sons of Hrethel thronged to the entrenchment. And there too, was Ongentheow, he the grey-haired King of the People driven to bay at the edge of the sword, and forced to submit to the sole doom of Eofor. And angrily did Wulf, son of Wanred, smite him with weapon, so that from that swinging blow blood-sweat gushed forth in streams under the hair of his head. Yet the old Swede was not terrified thereby, but quickly gave back a terrible blow by a worse exchange when the King of the people turned thither. Nor could Wulf the bold son of Wanred give back a blow to the old churl, for Ongentheow had formerly cut his helmet in two, so that he, stained with blood, fell prone perforce to the ground. But not yet was he doomed, but he raised himself up, though the wound touched him close. And the hardy thane of Hygelac (Eofor) when his brother lay prostrate, caused the broad sword, the old giant's sword, to crash through the wall of shields upon the gigantic helmet. Then stooped the King, the shepherd of the people, mortally wounded. And there were many who bound up his kinsman and quickly up-raised him when room had been made so that they might possess the battle-field, while one warrior was plundering another. One took the iron shield of Ongentheow, and his hard-hilted sword, and his helmet, and carried the trappings of the old man to Hygelac. And he received the treasures, and fairly he promised reward for the people, and he did as he promised. The lord of the Geats (Hygelac) son of Hrethel, re-

81   See Appendix IX.?

warded with very costly gifts the battle onset of Eofor and Wulf when he got back to his palace, and bestowed upon each of them a hundred thousand, of land and locked rings. Nor could any man in the world reproach him for that reward, since they had gained glory by fighting; and he gave to Eofor his only daughter, she who graced his homestead, to wed as a favour. And this is the feud and the enmity and hostile strife of men, which I expect the Swedish people will seek to awaken against us when they shall hear we have lost our Prince, he who in days of yore held treasure and kingdom against our foes after the fall of heroes, and held in check the fierce Swede, and did what was good for the people and deeds worthy of an earl. Now is it best for us to hasten to look upon our King and bring him who gave to us rings to the funeral pyre. Nor shall a part only of the treasure be melted with the proud man, but there is a hoard of wealth, an immense mass of gold, bought at a grim cost, for now at the very end of his life he bought for us rings. And the brands shall devour all the treasures and the flames of the funeral fire, they shall enfold them, nor shall an earl carry away any treasure as a memorial, nor shall any maid all beauteous wear on her neck ring adornments, but shall go sad of soul and bereft of gold, and often not once only tread an alien land now that the battle-wise man (Beowulf) has laid aside laughter, the games and the joys of song. And many a morning cold shall the spear in the hand-grip be heaved up on high, nor shall there be the sound of harping to awaken the warriors, but the war-raven, eager over the doomed ones, shall say many things to the eagle how it fared with him in eating the carrion while he, with the wolf, plundered the slaughtered.'

Thus then was the brave warrior reciting loathly spells. And he lied not at all in weird or word. Then the troop rose up together, and all unblithely went under Eagles' Ness, to look on the wonder, and tears were welling. Then they found him on the sand in his last resting-place, and bereft of soul, who had given them rings in days gone by, and then had the last day drawn to its close, for the good man Beowulf, the warrior King, the Lord of the Weder-Goths, had died a wondrous death.

But before this they had seen a more marvellous sight, the dragon on the sea-plain, the loathsome one lying right opposite. And there was the fire-dragon grimly terrible, and scorched with fire. And he was fifty feet in length as he lay there stretched out. He had had joy in the air awhile by night, but afterwards he went down to visit his den. But now he was the prisoner of death, and had enjoyed his last of earth-cares. And by him stood drinking-cups and flagons, and dishes were lying there and a costly sword, all rusty and eaten through as though they had rested a thousand winters in the bosom of the earth. And those heirlooms were fashioned so strongly, the gold of former races of men, and all wound round with spells, so that no man could come near that Ring-hall, unless God only, Himself the true King of victories, gave power to open up the hoard to whom He would (for He is the Protector of men) even to that man as it seemed good to Him.

FOURTY TWO

THEN WAS IT QUITE clear to them that the affair had not prospered with the monster, who had hidden ornaments within the cave under the cliff. The guardian thereof had slain some few in former days. Then had the feud been wrathfully avenged. And it is a mystery anywhere when a valiant earl reaches the end of his destiny, when a man may no longer with his kinsman dwell in the mead-hall. And thus was it with Beowulf when he sought out the guardian of the cavern and his cunning crafts. And he himself knew not how his departure from this world would come about. And thus famous chieftains uttered deep curses until the day of doom, because they had allowed it to come to pass that the monster should be guilty of such crimes, and, accursed and fast with hell-bands, as he was, and tormented with plagues that he should plunder the plain. He (Beowulf) was not greedy of gold, and had more readily in former days seen the favour of God.

Wiglaf spake, the son of Weohstan: 'Often shall many an earl of his own only will suffer misery, as is our fate. Nor could we teach the dear lord and shepherd of the kingdom any wisdom so that he would fail to be meeting the keeper of the gold treasures (the dragon) or to let him stay where he had been long time dwelling in his cavern until the world's end. But he held to his high destiny. Now the hoard is seen by us, grimly got hold of, and at too great a cost was it yielded to the King of the people whom he enticed to that conflict. I was within the cavern, and looked upon all the hoard, the decoration of the palace, when by no means pleasantly, room was made for me, and a faring was granted to me in under the sea-cliff. And in much haste I took a very great burden of hoard-treasures in my hand, and bore it forth hither to my King. He was still alive, wise and witting well. And he the ancient uttered many words in sadness, and bade me greet you, and commanded that ye should build after death of your friend a high grave-mound in the place of the funeral pyre, a great and famous monument, for he himself was the most worshipful of men throughout the earth, while he was enjoying the wealth of his city. Let us now go and see and seek yet once again the heap of treasures, the wonder under the cliff. I will direct you, so that ye may look at close quarters upon the rings and the wealth of gold. Let the bier be quickly made ready when we come forth again, and then let us carry the dear man our lord when he shall enjoy the protection of the Ruler of all things.'

Then the son of Weohstan, the battle-dear warrior, ordered that commandment should be given to many a hero and householder that they should bring the wood for the funeral pyre from far, they the folk-leaders, to where the good man lay dead.

'Now the war-flame shall wax and the fire shall eat up the strong chief among warriors, him who often endured the iron shower, when the storm of arrows, strongly impelled, shot over the shield-wall, and the shaft did good service, and all eager with its feather, fear followed and aided the barb.' Then the proud son of Weohstan summoned from the troop the thanes of the King, seven of them together, and the very best of them, and he the eighth went under the hostile roof. And one of the warriors carried in his hand a torch which went on in front.

And no wise was it allotted who should plunder that hoard, since they saw some part unguarded remaining in the Hall, and lying there fleeting.

And little did any man mourn when full heartily they carried forth the costly treasures. Then they shoved the dragon the worm over the cliff-wall, and let the wave take him and the flood embrace that guardian of the treasures. Then the twisted golden ornaments were loaded on a wagon, an immense number of them. And the noble Atheling, the hoar battle-warrior, was carried to Whales' Ness.

FOURTY THREE

THEN THE PEOPLE OF the Geats got ready the mighty funeral pyre, and hung it round with helmets and battle-shields, and bright byrnies as he had asked. And in the midst they lay the famous Prince, and they lamented the Hero, their dear lord. Then the warriors began to stir up the greatest of bale-fires on the cliff-side. And the reek of the wood-smoke went up swart, over the flame, which was resounding, and its roar mingled with weeping (and the tumult of winds was still), until it had broken the body, all hot into the heart. And unhappy in their thinkings, and with minds full of care, they proclaim the death of their lord, likewise a sorrowful song the Bride....[82]

And heaven swallowed up the smoke. Then on the cliff-slopes the people of the Geats erected a mound, very high and very broad, that it might be beholden from afar by the wave-farers; and they set up the beacon of the mighty in battle in ten days. And the leavings of the funeral fire they surrounded with a wall, so that very proud men might find it to be most worthy of reverence.

And they did on the barrow rings and necklaces, and all such adornments as formerly warlike men had taken of the hoard. And they allowed the earth to hold the treasure of earls, the gold on the ground, where it still is to be found as useless to men as it always was.[83] Then the battle-dear men rode round about the mound, the children of the Athelings, twelve of them there were in all, and would be uttering their sorrows and lamenting their King, and reciting a dirge, and speaking of their champion. And they talked of his earlship and of his brave works, and deemed them doughty, as is fitting that a man should praise his lord in words and cherish him in his heart when he shall have gone forth from the fleeting body. So the People of the Geats lamented over the fall of their lord, his hearth-companions, and said that he was a world-king, and the mildest, the gentlest of men, and most tender to his people, and most eager for their praise.

---

82   Text in MS. faulty here. Wyatt and Morris have adopted Bugge's emendation. The sense is that Beowulf's widow with her hair bound up utters forth a dirge over her dead husband.?

83   Probably the treasures that remained in the cavern. See previous chapter.?

Appendices

ONE
GENERAL NOTE ON THE POEM

THIS IS THE GREATEST poem that has come down to us from our Teutonic ancestors. Our only knowledge of it is through the unique MS. in the British Museum.

It has already been translated at least eight times as follows:

1. Kemble, 1837.
2. Thorpe and Arnold (with the O.E. Poem accompanying it).
3. Lumsden, 1881 (in ballad form).
4. Garnett, 1883.
5. Earle, 1892.
6. William Morris and A. J. Wyatt, 1895. This is in poetic form, but abounds in archaisms and difficult inversions, and is sometimes not easy to read or indeed to understand.
7. Wentworth Huyshe, 1907.
8. A translation in 1912. Author unknown.

Many of the persons and events of *Beowulf* are also known to us through various Scandinavian and French works as follows:

SCANDINAVIAN RECORDS.
1. Saxo's *Danish History*.
2. HrÓlf's *Saga Kraka*.
3. *Ynglinga Saga* (and *Ynglinga tÁl*).
4. *SkiÖldunga Saga*.

As instances of identical persons and events:
1. SkiÖldr, ancestor of SkiÖldungar, corresponds to Scyld the ancestor of Scyldungas.
2. The Danish King Halfdan corresponds to Healfdene.
3. His sons Hroarr and Helgi correspond to Hrothgar and Halga.
4. HrÖlf Kraki corresponds to Hrothwulf, nephew of Hrothgar.
5. Frothi corresponds to Froda, and his son Ingialdi to Ingeld.

6. Otarr corresponds to Ohthere, and his son Athils to Eadgils.

With the exception of the *Ynglinga tÁl* all these records are quite late, hence they do not afford any evidence for the dates of events mentioned in *Beowulf*.

Further Scandinavian correspondences are seen in BÖthvarr Biarki, the chief of HrÖlf Kraki's knights. He is supposed to correspond to Beowulf. He came to Leire, the Danish royal residence, and killed a demon in animal form. Saxo says it was a bear. This demon attacked the King's yard at Yule-tide, but Biarki and Beowulf differ as to their future, for Biarki stayed with HrÖlf Kraki to the end and died with him.

In the *Grettis Saga* the hero kills two demons, male and female. It is true that the scene is laid in Iceland, but minor details of scenery, the character of the demons, and other similarities make it impossible to believe the two stories to be different in origin. They both sprang out of a folk-tale associated after ten centuries with Grettis, and in England and Denmark with an historical prince of the Geats.

FRENCH RECORDS

1. *Historia Francorum* and *Gesta Regum Francorum* (discovered by Outzen and Leo).

In A.D. 520 a raid was made on the territory of the Chatuarii. Their king Theodberht, son of Theodric I, defeated Chocilaicus, who was killed. This Chocilaicus is identified with the Hygelac of our poem, and the raid with Hygelac's raid on the Hetware (= Chatuarii), the Franks, and the Frisians. This helps us to estimate the date for *Beowulf* as having been born somewhere about the end of the fifth century.

2. *Historia Francorum*, by Gregory of Tours. The author speaks of the raider as the King of the Danes.

3. *Liber Monstrorum*. In this work the raider is Rex Getarum, King of the Geats, who may correspond with the Geats of our poem. The Geats were the people of Gautland in Southern Sweden. See Appendix XI.

ORIGIN OF THE ANGLO-SAXON POEM

It was probably written in Northumbrian or Midland, but was preserved in a West Saxon translation.

There would seem to be some justifiable doubt as to the unity of the poem. Though on the whole pagan and primitive in tone, it has a considerable admixture of Christian elements, e.g. on pp. 29 and 30 and pp. 109–112, though the latter passage may be a late interpolation. Generally speaking, the poetry and sentiments are Christian in tone, but the customs are pagan. The author of the article in *The Cambridge History of English Literature*, vol. i., to whom I owe much, says: 'I cannot believe that any Christian poet could have composed the account of Beowulf's funeral.' One passage is very reminiscent of Eph. vi. 16, viz. Chapter XXV. p. 111; whilst page 25 (lower half) may be compared with CÆdmon's *Hymn*. There are also references to Cain and Abel and to the Deluge. Of Chapters I.–XXXI. the percentage of Christian elements is four, whilst of the remaining Chapters (XXXII. ad fin.) the percentage is ten, due chiefly to four long passages. Note especially that the words in Chapter II., 'And sometimes they went vowing at their heathen shrines and offered sacrifices,' et seq., are quite inconsistent with the Christian sentiment attributed to Hrothgar later in the poem. 'It is generally thought,' says the writer in *The Cambridge History of English Literature*, 'that several originally separate lays have been combined into one poem, and, while there is no proof of this, it is quite possible and not unlikely.'

There are in the poem four distinct lays:

1. Beowulf's Fight with Grendel.
2. Beowulf's Fight with Grendel's mother.
3. Beowulf's Return to the land of the Geats.
4. Beowulf's Fight with the Dragon.

Competent critics say that probably 1 and 2 ought to be taken together, while Beowulf's reception by Hygelac (see 3 above) is probably a separate lay. Some scholars have gone much further in the work of disintegration, even attributing one half of the poem to interpolators, whilst others suggest two parallel versions. Summing up, the writer in *The Cambridge History of English Literature* says: 'I am disposed to think that a large portion of the poem existed in epic form before the change of faith, and that the appearance of Christian elements in the poem is due to revision. The Christianity of *Beowulf* is of a singularly indefinite and individual type, which contrasts somewhat strongly with what is found in later Old English poetry. This revision must have been made at a very early date.'

The poem was built up between A.D. 512, the date of the famous raid of Hygelac (Chocilaicus) against the Hetware (Chatuarii), and 752, when the French Merovingian dynasty fell; for, says Arnold, 'The poem contains not a word which by any human ingenuity could be tortured into a reference to any event subsequent to the fall of the Merovingians' (A.D. 752).

TWO
THE PRELUDE

THE PRELUDE WOULD SEEM to be an attempt to link up the hero of the poem with the mythological progenitors of the Teutonic nations. Thomas Arnold says: 'That Sceaf, Scyld, and Beaw were among the legendary ancestors of the West Saxon line of kings no one disputes. But this does not mean much, for the poem itself shows that the same three were also among the legendary ancestors of the Danish kings.' Ethelward, who wrote early in the tenth century, gives the ancestry of Ethelwulf, the father of Alfred. Ethelward says: 'The seventeenth ancestor from Cerdic was Beo, the eighteenth Scyld, the nineteenth Scef.' Ethelward also says: 'Scef himself, with one light vessel, arrived in the island of the ocean which is called Scani, dressed in armour, and he was a very young boy, and the inhabitants of that land knew nothing about him; however, he was received by them, and kept with care and affection as though he were of their own kin, and afterwards they chose him to be king, from whose stock the King Athulf [Ethelwulf] derives his line.'

It may be noted that neither Scyld nor Scef is mentioned in the A.S. Chronicle (A.D. 855). William of Malmesbury, in his Gesta Regum, says that Scef was so called from the sheaf of wheat that lay at his head, that he was asleep when he arrived, and that when he grew up he became a king in the town then called Slaswic, now Haithebi (Rolls Ed., 1. 121).

MÜllenhoff says: 'If we look closely into the saga, the ship and the sheaf clearly point to navigation and agriculture, the arms and jewels to kingly rule – all four gifts, therefore, to the main elements and foundations of the oldest state of culture among the Germans [Teutons?] of the sea-board; and if the bearer of these symbols became the first king of the country, the meaning can only be this, that from his appearance the beginning of the oldest state of culture dates, and that generally before him no orderly way of leading a human life had existed.'

Scyld (meaning Shield) refers to the fact that the king was the protector of the people in war, and is therefore symbolical, like Scef.

The ship and the sheaf, the arms and the jewels and the shield – these are the symbols of that primitive civilization – the sheaf, the symbol of agriculture and food, the ship of commerce, the arms of warfare, the jewels of reward of bravery, and the shield of the protection of the people by the king.

Arnold mentions the fact that no writer not English mentions the saga of Scef and Scyld, and suggests that this is presumption for the

English origin of the legend. I do not, however, think it is conclusive evidence. One is surprised that they are not mentioned in Icelandic literature. Yet somehow the impression on my mind is that these legends were probably brought by our Saxon and Danish ancestors from the Continent, and are taken for granted as well known to the hearers of the song. I think they probably formed part of the legendary genealogy of our common Germanic (Teutonic) ancestors, and happened to find their way into literature only among the English, or have survived only in the English.

THREE
'BROSINGA MENE'

'Brosinga Mene,' p. 82, is the 'Brisinga-mÉn' mentioned in the *Edda*, an Icelandic poem. 'This necklace is the Brisinga-mÉn – the costly necklace of Freja, which she won from the Dwarfs, and which was stolen from her by Loki, as is told in the *Edda*' (Kemble).

Loki was a Scandinavian demi-god. He was beautiful and cunning. He was the principle of strife, the spirit of evil; cp. Job's Satan. Freya was the Scandinavian Goddess of Love. She claimed half of the slain in battle. She was the dispenser of joy and happiness. The German *frau* is derived from Freya. Hama carried off this necklace when he fled from Eormanric. The origin of this legend, though worked up in the *Edda*, seems to have been German or Gothic, and 'Brosinga' has reference to the rock-plateau of Breisgau on the Rhine. It is probably a relic of the lost saga of Eormanric (see Appendix IV.), the famous Ostrogothic king referred to in Chapter XVIII. Eormanric is one of the few historical personages of the poem.

FOUR
EORMANRIC

Gibbon mentions Eormanric in his chapter XXV. of the *Decline and Fall*, and, in spite of chronological discrepancies, this Eormanric is probably identical with the one mentioned in *Beowulf* (Chapter XVIII.), in Jornandes (Chapter XXIV.), and in the *Edda*.

In Jornandes the story is as follows.

Characters

1. Ermanaric.

2. A Chief of the Roxolani tribe who was a traitor.

3. Sanielh (= Swanhild) wife of the chief.

4. Sarus,
5. Ammius, } brothers of Sanielh.

Ermanaric puts Sanielh to death by causing her to be torn to pieces by wild horses, because of the treachery of her husband, the chief of the Roxolani. Her brothers, Ammius and Sarus, avenge her death by attacking Ermanaric, but they only succeed in wounding him and disabling him for the rest of his life.

In the *Edda* the story is as follows.

Characters

1. Gudrun, widow of Sigurd and Atli.
2. Swanhild, daughter of Gudrun by Sigurd.
3. Jonakur, Gudrun's third husband.
4. SÖrli,
5. Hamthir, } sons of Gudrun and Jonakur.
6. Erp,
7. Jormunrek (Eormanric).
8. Randver, son of Jormunrek.

Jormunrek hears of the beauty of Swanhild and sends his son Randver to seek her out for him in marriage. Gudrun consents; on the way Randver is incited by the traitor Bicci to betray Swanhild, and is then accused by him to the king. For this treachery Jormunrek hangs Randver and causes Swanhild to be trampled to death by wild horses. Then the three sons of Gudrun set out to avenge their sister. On the way his two brothers kill Erp, and are consequently unable to kill Jormunrek. They only succeed in maiming him.

Saxo Grammaticus, to whom we also owe the story of Hamlet, tells a similar story.

Characters

1. Jarmeric, a Danish King.
2. Swawilda (= Swanhild), wife of Jarmeric.
3. Hellespontine brothers, brothers of Swawilda.
4. Bicco, a servant of Jarmeric.

Bicco accuses Swawilda to Jarmeric of unfaithfulness. He causes her to be torn to pieces by wild horses. Then her brothers kill Jarmeric with the help of a witch, Gudrun, hewing off his hands and feet.

These three stories are evidently based on one common original.

FIVE
MARRIAGE OF FREAWARU AND INGELD

Characters
1. Freawaru, daughter of Hrothgar the Dane.
2. Ingeld, son of Froda, King of the Heathobards.
3. Froda, King of the Heathobards.
4. A Heathobard warrior.
5. Son of the Danish warrior who had killed Froda.

The Heathobards were a people in Zealand. There had been an ancient feud between the Danes and the Heathobards in which Froda had been killed by a Danish warrior. Hrothgar hoped to appease the feud by the marriage of his daughter Freawaru to Ingeld. Unluckily, the son of the Danish warrior who had killed Froda accompanied Freawaru to Ingeld's Court. Then an old Heathobard warrior notices this and stirs up strife. The marriage fails in its object, and war breaks out again between the Danes and the Heathobards. Beowulf predicts the course of events in his speech to Hygelac (Chapters XXVIII. and XXIX.).

SIX
FINN

THE FINN EPISODE (Chapters XVI. and XVII.) is one of those events in *Beowulf* that would be quite well known to the first hearers of the song, but to us is lacking in that clearness we might desire. Fortunately, Dr. Hickes discovered a fragment entitled, 'The Fight at Finnsburgh,' on the back of a MS. of the *Homilies*. From *Beowulf* and from this fragment we are able to piece together an intelligible story. It is probably as follows:
Characters
1. Finn, King of the North Frisians and Jutes.
2. Hoc, a Danish chieftain.
3. Hildeburh, daughter of Hoc.
4. Hnaef, son of Hoc.
5. Hengest, son of Hoc.
6. Two sons of Finn and Hildeburh.
7. Hunlafing, a Finnish warrior.
8. Guthlaf and Oslaf, two Danish warriors.

Finn abducts Hildeburh, the daughter of Hoc, the Dane. Hoc pursues the two fugitives and is killed in the mÊlÉe. Twenty years pass by – Hnaef and Hengest, sons of Hoc, take up the 'vendetta.' In the fighting Hnaef and a son of Finn and Hildeburh are slain. A peace is patched up. Hengest, son of Hoc, is persuaded to remain as a guest of Finn for the winter, and it is agreed that no reference shall be made by either side to the feud between them. Then the bodies of Hnaef, Hildeburh's brother, and of her son are burnt together on the funeral pyre, 'and great is the mourning of Hildeburh for her son.' But Hengest is ever brooding vengeance. The strife breaks out anew in the spring. Hengest is killed, but two of his warriors, Guthlaf and Oslaf, break through the enemy, return to Finn's country, and slay him and carry off Hildeburh. 'The Fight at Finnsburgh,' which is Homeric in style, is the account of the first invasion of Finn by Hnaef and Hengest, and Wyatt fits it in before the Finn episode on p. 75. MÖller places it after the phrase, 'whose edge was well known to the Jutes,' on p. 79.

VII
HYGELAC

HYGELAC, SON OF HRETHEL, was king of the Geats, and uncle of Beowulf, his sister's son. He was the reigning king of Beowulf's fellow countrymen the Geats during the greater part of the action of the poem. Beowulf is often called 'Hygelac's kinsman,' and when he went forth to his battle with Grendel's mother (Chapter XXII.), he bade Hrothgar in case of his death send the treasures he had given to him to Hygelac. Hygelac married Hygd, who is presented to us as a good Queen, the daughter of HÆreth. She was 'very young,' 'of noble character,' and 'wise.' She is compared, to her advantage, with Thrytho, who was a shrewish woman. No one dared to look upon her except her husband. However, her second husband, Offa, seems to have 'tamed the shrew' (see p. 120). Hygelac has been identified with Chocilaicus, who was killed in the famous raid on the Chatuarii referred to in the *Historia Francorum* and the *Gesta Regum*, who are identified with the Hetware of this poem (see p. 143 and Appendix I.).

The famous raid of Hygelac upon the Hetware in which he met his death is referred to five times in the poem, as follows: Chapters XVIII., p. 83; XXXI., p. 134; XXXIII., p. 142; XXXV., p. 151; XL., p. 172.

On the death of Hygelac his son Heardred succeeded to the throne (Chapter XXXI., p. 134); and, after a brief interval, he was killed in battle by Onela (see Appendix IX.). Then Beowulf succeeded to the throne of the Geats (Chapter XXXI., p. 134). Hygelac died between a.d. 512 and 520. Beowulf died about 568. He reigned fifty years.

EIGHT
HÆTHCYN AND HEREBALD

IT WOULD SEEM DOUBTFUL as to whether this was deliberate or accidental. The poet says 'HÆthcyn missed the mark' with his javelin and killed his brother Herebald; but subsequently he speaks as though it had been deliberate murder.

NINE
WARS BETWEEN THE SWEDES AND THE GEATS

Characters
1. *Swedes*
    1. Ongentheow, King of the Swedes.
    2. Onthere, } his two sons.
    3. Onela,
    4. Eadgils, } two sons of Ohthere.
    5. Eanmund,

2. *Geats, &c.*
    6. HÆthcyn, King of Geats.
    7. Hygelac, King of Geats.
    8. Heardred, King of Geats.
    9. Beowulf, King of Geats.
    10. Eofor, } two Geat warriors.
    11. Wulf,

Ongentheow was a King of the Swedes. The Swedes are also called Scylfings in the poem. The origin of the word 'Scylfing' is doubtful. Ongentheow went to war with HÆthcyn, King of the Geats and brother of Hygelac; and Ongentheow, who was well advanced in years, struck down his foe (Chapter XL., p. 173) at the battle of Ravenswood. This was the first time that the Swedes invaded the Geats. The Geats retreated into the Ravenswood at nightfall, but with the dawn they heard the horn of Hygelac 'as the good prince came marching on the track.'

Ongentheow now was alarmed, for Hygelac's prowess in battle was far-famed. He withdrew into some fortification, and was attacked by the Geats. Two brothers, Eofor and Wulf, assailed the veteran warrior. He defended himself with great vigour and killed Wulf; but Eofor came to the help of his brother and dealt Ongentheow his death-blow over the guard of his shield.

Ongentheow's two sons were Onela and Ohthere. Ohthere had two sons, Eanmund and Eadgils.

These two sons of Ohthere were banished from Sweden for rebellion, and took refuge at the Court of the Geat King Heardred. This great-ly enraged their uncle Onela, that they should resort to the Court of their hereditary foes (see above). Onela invaded the land of the Geats (Chapters XXXIII. and XXXIV., pp. 144 sq.) and slew Heardred. Then it was that Beowulf became King of the Geats. Thus two Geatish kings had been slain by the Swedes, viz. HÆthcyn and Heardred. In revenge, later on, Beowulf supported Eadgils in his counter-attack on his own fatherland when Eadgils killed his uncle Onela. This story is confirmed by the Scandinavian accounts in which Athils (= Eadgils) slew Ali (= Onela) on the ice of Lake Wener; cp. the phrase 'cold journeyings' (Chapter XXXIV., p. 145).

This is Wyatt's version of the story.

TEN
SIGMUND

SIGMUND (PAGE 65) IS the father and uncle of Fitela. He is stated in *Be-owulf* to have killed a serpent who kept guard over a hoard of treasure. In the Icelandic saga known as the *Völsunga Saga*, Sigmund is repre-sented as the father of Sigurd, and 'it is Sigurd who rifles the treasure of the Niblungs and kills the serpent (Fafnir), its guardian' (Arnold, p. 69), and he carries it away on the back of his horse Grani. Sigmund is represented as the son of a Völsung; that is, as *Beowulf* has it, 'the heir of Waels.' Waels was afterwards forgotten, however, and Waelsing was regarded as a proper name instead of a patronymic denoting descent from Waels. In a similar way, as Arnold points out, Sigmund is pushed into the background to make room for his son Sigurd (Siegfried). 'And so in the German *Nibelungen Lay* it is Sigurd (Siegfried) who wins the hoard, but does so by defeating and killing its former possessors Schil-bung and Nibelung' (Arnold, p. 70). Attempts have been made to claim a German origin for this saga, but in face of the evidence of *Beowulf* and the *Völsunga Saga* and the *Edda* there is, I think with Arnold, little doubt but that its origin was Scandinavian. Possibly and probably we owe the later elaboration of the saga in the *Nibelungen Lay* to German influence. For discussion of the whole question see Arnold's *Notes on Beowulf*, pp. 67–75, Edit. 1898, cap. v.

ELEVEN
TRIBES MENTIONED IN THE POEM

1. *Brondings*. Breca was a Bronding. After his famous swimming-match with Beowulf (Chapter VIII.), he is said to have sought out his 'pleasant fatherland the land of the Brondings.' Arnold suggests that they were located in Mecklenburg or Pomerania.

2. *Danes*, also called Bright-Danes, Ring-Danes, Spear-Danes, because of their warlike character; and North Danes, South Danes, &c., because of their wide distribution. They are said to have inhabited the Scede lands and Scedenig and 'between the seas'; that is, they were spread over the Danish Islands, the southern province of Sweden, and the seas between them.

3. *Jutes* (Eotenas), probably people ruled over by Finn, King of Friesland, and identical with the Frisians.

4. *Franks* and Frisians. The Franks were ancestors of the modern French. After the conversion of Clovis (A.D. 496), they gradually encroached on the Frisians.

5. *Frisians* include the Frisians, the Franks, the Hetware, and the Hugs. Friesland was the country between the River Ems and the Zuyder Zee.

6. *Geats*. They dwelt in the south of Sweden between the Danes and the Swedes. Bugge sought to identify them with the Jutes, and held that Gautland was Juteland. He based this theory on certain phrases: e.g. Chapter XXXIII., where the Swedes (the sons of Ohthere) are said to have visited the Geats 'across the sea,' and again in Chapter XXXV. the Swedes and the Geats are said to have fought 'over wide water'; but, as Arnold points out, these phrases can be interpreted in such a way as not to be incompatible with the theory that they dwelt on the same side of the Cattegat, i.e. on the northern side, and in the extreme south of Sweden.

The question as to whether they are identical with the Goths of Roman history is still an open one. Arnold says, 'There is a great weight of evidence tending to identify the Geats with the Goths,' and he quotes evidence from Gibbon (chapter X.). Pytheas of Marseilles, in the fourth century, says that, passing through the Baltic Sea, he met with tribes of Goths, Teutons, and Ests.

Tacitus, in chapter XLIII. of *Germania*, speaks of the Goths as dwelling near the Swedes. Jornandes traces the Goths to Scanzia, an island in the Northern Sea. It is probable, then, that the Goths had a northern and indeed a Scandinavian origin. If so, Beowulf the Geat was probably a Goth.

7. *Healfdenes.* The tribe to which Hnaef belonged.

8. *Heathoremes.* The people on whose shores Beowulf was cast up after his swimming-match with Breca.

9. *Ingwine.* Friends of Ing – another name for the Danes.

10. *Scyldingas.* Another name for the Danes, as descended from Scyld.

11. *Scylfingas.* Name for the Swedes.

12. *Waegmundings.* The tribe to which both Beowulf and Wiglaf belonged.

13. *Wylfings.* Probably a Gothic tribe.

TWELVE

THE TEXT HERE IS much mutilated, and can only be restored by ingenious conjecture. Grein and Bugge and others have reconstructed it. On the whole Bugge's text, which I have followed, seems to me the most reasonable. It is unfortunate that the text should be so imperfect just at this critical point in the linking up of the two great divisions of the story. In the ancient days some remote predecessors of the Geats seem to have heaped up in the neighbourhood a pile of wonderful vessels jewel-bedecked, and treasures of all kinds, of inconceivable value. Then the last of the race carries the treasure to a barrow or cavern in the cliffs near the site, in after-generations, of Beowulf's palace, and delivers a pathetic farewell address (pp. 136 et seq.). The dragon finds the cavern and the treasure and appropriates it for three hundred years. Then one of Beowulf's retainers finds the treasure and takes a golden goblet while the dragon is sleeping, and offers it to his lord as a peace-offering. This brought about Beowulf's feud with the dragon in which he met his death.

Books Consulted

BEOWULF, EDITED WITH textual footnotes, &c., by A. J. Wyatt, M.A. (Cantab. and London). Pitt Press, Cambridge, 1898.

Zupitza's Transliteration of Beowulf. A photographic reproduction of the manuscript. Early English Text Society.

Encyclopaedia Britannica.

Chambers's Encyclopaedia.

Beowulf, Notes on, by Thomas Arnold, M.A., 1898. Longmans, Green & Co. This contains a good map of the scenes alluded to in the poem.

History of Early English Literature, by the Rev. Stopford Brooke.

Ten Brink's *English Literature.*

BEOWULF
IN VERSE

John Lesslie Hall

PREFACE

THE PRESENT WORK is a modest effort to reproduce approximately, in modern measures, the venerable epic, *Beowulf*. *Approximately*, I repeat; for a very close reproduction of Anglo-Saxon verse would, to a large extent, be prose to a modern ear.

The Heyne-Socin text and glossary have been closely followed. Occasionally a deviation has been made, but always for what seemed good and sufficient reason. The translator does not aim to be an editor. Once in a while, however, he has added a conjecture of his own to the emendations quoted from the criticisms of other students of the poem.

This work is addressed to two classes of readers. From both of these alike the translator begs sympathy and co-operation. The Anglo-Saxon scholar he hopes to please by adhering faithfully to the original. The student of English literature he aims to interest by giving him, in modern garb, the most ancient epic of our race. This is a bold and venturesome undertaking; and yet there must be some students of the Teutonic past willing to follow even a daring guide, if they may read in modern phrases of the sorrows of Hrothgar, of the prowess of Beowulf, and of the feelings that stirred the hearts of our forefathers in their primeval homes.

In order to please the larger class of readers, a regular cadence has been used, a measure which, while retaining the essential characteristics of the original, permits the reader to see ahead of him in reading.

Perhaps every Anglo-Saxon scholar has his own theory as to how *Beowulf* should be translated. Some have given us prose versions of what we believe to be a great poem. Is it any reflection on our honored Kemble and Arnold to say that their translations fail to show a layman that *Beowulf* is justly called our first *epic*? Of those translators who have used verse, several have written from what would seem a mistaken point of view. Is it proper, for instance, that the grave and solemn speeches of Beowulf and Hrothgar be put in ballad measures, tripping lightly and airily along? Or, again, is it fitting that the rough martial music of Anglo-Saxon verse be interpreted to us in the smooth measures of modern blank verse? Do we hear what has been beautifully called "the clanging tread of a warrior in mail"?

Of all English translations of *Beowulf*, that of Professor Garnett alone gives any adequate idea of the chief characteristics of this great Teutonic epic.

The measure used in the present translation is believed to be as near a reproduction of the original as modern English affords. The cadences closely resemble those used by Browning in some of his most striking poems. The four stresses of the Anglo-Saxon verse are retained, and as much thesis and anacrusis is allowed as is consistent with a regular cadence. Alliteration has been used to a large extent; but it was thought that modern ears would hardly tolerate it on every line. End-rhyme has been used occasionally; internal rhyme, sporadically. Both have some warrant in Anglo-Saxon poetry.

What Gummere[1] calls the "rime-giver" has been studiously kept; viz., the first accented syllable in the second half-verse always carries the alliteration; and the last accented syllable alliterates only sporadically. Alternate alliteration is occasionally used as in the original.

No two accented syllables have been brought together, except occasionally after a caesural pause. Or, scientifically speaking, Sievers's C type has been avoided as not consonant with the plan of translation. Several of his types, however, constantly occur; e.g. A and a variant (/ × | / ×) (/ × × | / ×); B and a variant (× / | × /) (× × / | × /); a variant of D (/ × | / × ×); E (/ × × | /). Anacrusis gives further variety to the types used in the translation.

The parallelisms of the original have been faithfully preserved. "Lord" and "Wielder of Glory"; Occasionally, some loss has been sustained; but, on the other hand, a gain has here and there been made.

The effort has been made to give a decided flavor of archaism to the translation. All words not in keeping with the spirit of the poem have been avoided. Again, though many archaic words have been used, there are none, it is believed, which are not found in standard modern poetry.

With these preliminary remarks, it will not be amiss to give an outline of the story of the poem.

---

1   *Handbook of Poetics*, page 175, 1st edition.

THE STORY

HROTHGAR, king of the Danes, or Scyldings, builds a great mead hall, or palace, in which he hopes to feast his liegemen and to give them presents. The joy of king and retainers is, however, of short duration. Grendel, the monster, is seized with hateful jealousy. He cannot brook the sounds of joyance that reach him down in his fen-dwelling near the hall. Oft and anon he goes to the joyous building, bent on direful mischief. Thane after thane is ruthlessly carried off and devoured, while no one is found strong enough and bold enough to cope with the monster. For twelve years he persecutes Hrothgar and his vassals.

Over sea, a day's voyage off, Beowulf, of the Geats, nephew of Higelac, king of the Geats, hears of Grendel's doings and of Hrothgar's misery. He resolves to crush the fell monster and relieve the aged king. With fourteen chosen companions, he sets sail for Daneland. Reaching that country, he soon persuades Hrothgar of his ability to help him. The hours that elapse before night are spent in beer-drinking and conversation. When Hrothgar's bedtime comes he leaves the hall in charge of Beowulf, telling him that never before has he given to another the absolute wardship of his palace. All retire to rest, Beowulf, as it were, sleeping upon his arms.

Grendel comes, the great march-stepper, bearing God's anger. He seizes and kills one of the sleeping warriors. Then he advances towards Beowulf. A fierce and desperate hand-to-hand struggle ensues. No arms are used, both combatants trusting to strength and hand-grip. Beowulf tears Grendel's shoulder from its socket, and the monster retreats to his den, howling and yelling with agony and fury. The wound is fatal.

The next morning, at early dawn, warriors in numbers flock to the hall Heorot, to hear the news. Joy is boundless. Glee runs high. Hrothgar and his retainers are lavish of gratitude and of gifts.

Grendel's mother, however, comes the next night to avenge his death.

She is furious and raging. While Beowulf is sleeping in a room some-what apart from the quarters of the other warriors, she seizes one of Hrothgar's favorite counsellors, and carries him off and devours him. Beowulf is called. Determined to leave Heorot entirely purified, he arms himself, and goes down to look for the female monster. After traveling through the waters many hours, he meets her near the sea bottom. She drags him to her den. There he sees Grendel lying dead. After a desper-ate and almost fatal struggle with the woman, he slays her, and swims upward in triumph, taking with him Grendel's head.

Joy is renewed at Heorot. Congratulations crowd upon the victor. Hrothgar literally pours treasures into the lap of Beowulf; and it is agreed among the vassals of the king that Beowulf will be their next liege lord.

Beowulf leaves Daneland. Hrothgar weeps and laments at his depar-ture.

When the hero arrives in his own land, Higelac treats him as a distin-guished guest. He is the hero of the hour.

Beowulf subsequently becomes king of his own people, the Geats. After he has been ruling for fifty years, his own neighborhood is woe-fully harried by a fire-spewing dragon. Beowulf determines to kill him. In the ensuing struggle both Beowulf and the dragon are slain. The grief of the Geats is inexpressible. They determine, however, to leave nothing undone to honor the memory of their lord. A great funeral pyre is built, and his body is burnt. Then a memorial-barrow is made, visible from a great distance, that sailors afar may be constantly reminded of the prowess of the national hero of Geatland.

The poem closes with a glowing tribute to his bravery, his gentleness, his goodness of heart, and his generosity.

It is the devout desire of this translator to hasten the day when the story of Beowulf shall be as familiar to English-speaking peoples as that of the *Iliad*. *Beowulf* is our first great epic. It is an epitomized history of the life of the Teutonic races. It brings vividly before us our forefathers of pre-Alfredian eras, in their love of war, of sea, and of adventure.

My special thanks are due to Professors Francis A. March and James A. Harrison, for advice, sympathy, and assistance.

J. L. Hall.

Williamsburg, VA, Nov. 1, 1891.

ONE

The Life and Death of Scyld

LO! THE SPEAR-DANES' glory through splendid achievements
The folk-kings' former fame we have heard of,
How princes displayed then their prowess-in-battle.
Oft Scyld the Scefing from scathers in numbers
From many a people their mead-benches tore.
Since first he found him friendless and wretched,
The earl had had terror: comfort he got for it,
Waxed 'neath the welkin, world-honor gained,
Till all his neighbors o'er sea were compelled to
Bow to his bidding and bring him their tribute:
An excellent atheling![2] After was borne him
A son and heir, young in his dwelling,
Whom God-Father sent to solace the people.
He had marked the misery malice had caused them,
That reaved of their rulers they wretched had erstwhile
Long been afflicted. The Lord, in requital,
Wielder[3] of Glory, with world-honor blessed him.
Famed was Beowulf, far spread the glory
Of Scyld's great son in the lands of the Danemen.
So the carle[4] that is young, by kindnesses rendered
The friends of his father, with fees in abundance
Must be able to earn that when age approacheth
Eager companions aid him requitingly,
When war assaults him serve him as liegemen:

2   Prince, nobleman.
3   Ruler. Often used of God.
4   Man, hero.

By praise-worthy actions must honor be got
'Mong all of the races. At the hour that was fated
Scyld then departed to the All-Father's keeping
Warlike to wend him; away then they bare him
To the flood of the current, his fond-loving comrades,
As himself he had bidden, while the friend of the Scyldings
Word-sway wielded, and the well-lovèd land-prince
Long did rule them. The ring-stemmèd vessel,
Bark of the atheling, lay there at anchor,
Icy in glimmer and eager for sailing;
The belovèd leader laid they down there,
Giver of rings, on the breast of the vessel,
The famed by the mainmast. A many of jewels,
Of fretted embossings, from far-lands brought over,
Was placed near at hand then; and heard I not ever
That a folk ever furnished a float[5] more superbly
With weapons of warfare, weeds for the battle,
Bills[6] and burnies;[7] on his bosom sparkled
Many a jewel that with him must travel
On the flush of the flood afar on the current.
And favors no fewer they furnished him soothly,
Excellent folk-gems, than others had given him
Who when first he was born outward did send him
Lone on the main, the merest of infants:
And a gold-fashioned standard they stretched under heaven
High o'er his head, let the holm-currents[8] bear him,
Seaward consigned him: sad was their spirit,
Their mood very mournful. Men are not able
Soothly to tell us, they in halls who reside,
Heroes under heaven, to what haven he hied.

---

5   Vessel, ship.
6   Swords.
7   Armor.
8   Ocean, curved surface of the sea.

TWO

Scyld's Successors – Hrothgar's Great Mead-Hall

IN THE BOROUGHS then Beowulf, bairn of the Scyldings,
Belovèd land-prince, for long-lasting season
Was famed mid the folk (his father departed,
The prince from his dwelling), till afterward sprang
Great-minded Healfdene; the Danes in his lifetime
He graciously governed, grim-mooded, agèd.
Four bairns of his body born in succession
Woke in the world, war-troopers' leader
Heorogar, Hrothgar, and Halga the good;
Heard I that Elan was Ongentheow's consort,
The well-beloved bedmate of the War-Scylfing leader.
Then glory in battle to Hrothgar was given,
Waxing of war-fame, that willingly kinsmen
Obeyed his bidding, till the boys grew to manhood,
A numerous band. It burned in his spirit
To urge his folk to found a great building,
A mead-hall grander than men of the era
Ever had heard of, and in it to share
With young and old all of the blessings
The Lord had allowed him, save life and retainers.
Then the work I find afar was assigned
To many races in middle-earth's regions,
To adorn the great folk-hall. In due time it happened
Early 'mong men, that 'twas finished entirely,
The greatest of hall-buildings; Heorot he named it

Who wide-reaching word-sway wielded 'mong earlmen.
His promise he brake not, rings he lavished,
Treasure at banquet. Towered the hall up
High and horn-crested, huge between antlers:
It battle-waves bided, the blasting fire-demon;
Ere long then from hottest hatred must sword-wrath
Arise for a woman's husband and father.
Then the mighty war-spirit endured for a season,
Bore it bitterly, he who bided in darkness,
That light-hearted laughter loud in the building
Greeted him daily; there was dulcet harp-music,
Clear song of the singer. He said that was able
To tell from of old earthmen's beginnings,
That Father Almighty earth had created,
The winsome wold[9] that the water encircleth,
Set exultingly the sun's and the moon's beams
To lavish their lustre on land-folk and races,
And earth He embellished in all her regions
With limbs and leaves; life He bestowed too
On all the kindreds that live under heaven.
So blessed with abundance, brimming with joyance,
The warriors abided, till a certain one gan to
Dog them with deeds of direfullest malice,
A foe in the hall-building: this horrible stranger
Was Grendel entitled, the march-stepper famous
Who dwelt in the moor-fens, the marsh and the fastness;
The wan-mooded being abode for a season
In the land of the giants, when the Lord and Creator
Had banned him and branded. For that bitter murder,
The killing of Abel, all-ruling Father
The kindred of Cain crushed with His vengeance;
In the feud He rejoiced not, but far away drove him
From kindred and kind, that crime to atone for,
Meter of Justice. Thence ill-favored creatures,
Elves and giants, monsters of ocean,
Came into being, and the giants that longtime
Grappled with God; He gave them requital.

9   Plane, extended surface.

THREE

Grendel the Murderer

WHEN THE SUN was sunken, he set out to visit
The lofty hall-building, how the Ring-Danes had used it
For beds and benches when the banquet was over.
Then he found there reposing many a noble
Asleep after supper; sorrow the heroes,
Misery knew not. The monster of evil
Greedy and cruel tarried but little,
Fell and frantic, and forced from their slumbers
Thirty of thanemen; thence he departed
Leaping and laughing, his lair to return to,
With surfeit of slaughter sallying homeward.
In the dusk of the dawning, as the day was just breaking,
Was Grendel's prowess revealed to the warriors:
Then, his meal-taking finished, a moan was uplifted,
Morning-cry mighty. The man-ruler famous,
The long-worthy atheling, sat very woeful,
Suffered great sorrow, sighed for his liegemen,
When they had seen the track of the hateful pursuer,
The spirit accursèd: too crushing that sorrow,
Too loathsome and lasting. Not longer he tarried,
But one night after continued his slaughter
Shameless and shocking, shrinking but little
From malice and murder; they mastered him fully.
He was easy to find then who otherwhere looked for
A pleasanter place of repose in the lodges,
A bed in the bowers. Then was brought to his notice
Told him truly by token apparent

The hall-thane's hatred: he held himself after
Further and faster who the foeman did baffle.
So ruled he and strongly strove against justice
Lone against all men, till empty uptowered
The choicest of houses. Long was the season:
Twelve-winters' time torture suffered
The friend of the Scyldings, every affliction,
Endless agony; hence it after became
Certainly known to the children of men
Sadly in measures, that long against Hrothgar
Grendel struggled: – his grudges he cherished,
Murderous malice, many a winter,
Strife unremitting, and peacefully wished he
Life-woe to lift from no liegeman at all of
The men of the Dane-folk, for money to settle,
No counsellor needed count for a moment
On handsome amends at the hands of the murderer;
The monster of evil fiercely did harass,
The ill-planning death-shade, both elder and younger,
Trapping and tricking them. He trod every night then
The mist-covered moor-fens; men do not know where
Witches and wizards wander and ramble.
So the foe of mankind many of evils
Grievous injuries, often accomplished,
Horrible hermit; Heort he frequented,
Gem-bedecked palace, when night-shades had fallen
(Since God did oppose him, not the throne could he touch,
The light-flashing jewel, love of Him knew not).
'Twas a fearful affliction to the friend of the Scyldings
Soul-crushing sorrow. Not seldom in private
Sat the king in his council; conference held they
What the braves should determine 'gainst terrors unlooked for.
At the shrines of their idols often they promised
Gifts and offerings, earnestly prayed they
The devil from hell would help them to lighten
Their people's oppression. Such practice they used then,
Hope of the heathen; hell they remembered
In innermost spirit, God they knew not,
Judge of their actions, All-wielding Ruler,
No praise could they give the Guardian of Heaven,
The Wielder of Glory. Woe will be his who

Through furious hatred his spirit shall drive to
The clutch of the fire, no comfort shall look for,
Wax no wiser; well for the man who,
Living his life-days, his Lord may face
And find defence in his Father's embrace!

FOUR

Beowulf Goes to Hrothgar's Assistance

So HEALFDENE'S KINSMAN constantly mused on
His long-lasting sorrow; the battle-thane clever
Was not anywise able evils to 'scape from:
Too crushing the sorrow that came to the people,
Loathsome and lasting the life-grinding torture,
Greatest of night-woes. So Higelac's liegeman,
Good amid Geatmen, of Grendel's achievements
Heard in his home: of heroes then living
He was stoutest and strongest, sturdy and noble.
He bade them prepare him a bark that was trusty;
He said he the war-king would seek o'er the ocean,
The folk-leader noble, since he needed retainers.
For the perilous project prudent companions
Chided him little, though loving him dearly;
They egged the brave atheling, augured him glory.
The excellent knight from the folk of the Geatmen
Had liegemen selected, likest to prove them
Trustworthy warriors; with fourteen companions
The vessel he looked for; a liegeman then showed them,
A sea-crafty man, the bounds of the country.
Fast the days fleeted; the float was a-water,
The craft by the cliff. Clomb to the prow then
Well-equipped warriors: the wave-currents twisted
The sea on the sand; soldiers then carried
On the breast of the vessel bright-shining jewels,

Handsome war-armor; heroes outshoved then,
Warmen the wood-ship, on its wished-for adventure.
The foamy-necked floater fanned by the breeze,
Likest a bird, glided the waters,
Till twenty and four hours thereafter
The twist-stemmed vessel had traveled such distance
That the sailing-men saw the sloping embankments,
The sea cliffs gleaming, precipitous mountains,
Nesses[10] enormous: they were nearing the limits
At the end of the ocean. Up thence quickly
The men of the Weders clomb to the mainland,
Fastened their vessel (battle weeds rattled,
War burnies clattered), the Wielder they thanked
That the ways o'er the waters had waxen so gentle.
Then well from the cliff edge the guard of the Scyldings
Who the sea-cliffs should see to, saw o'er the gangway
Brave ones bearing beauteous targets,
Armor all ready, anxiously thought he,
Musing and wondering what men were approaching.
High on his horse then Hrothgar's retainer
Turned him to coastward, mightily brandished
His lance in his hands, questioned with boldness.
"Who are ye men here, mail-covered warriors
Clad in your corslets, come thus a-driving
A high riding ship o'er the shoals of the waters,
And hither 'neath helmets have hied o'er the ocean?
I have been strand-guard, standing as warden,
Lest enemies ever anywise ravage
Danish dominions with army of war-ships.
More boldly never have warriors ventured
Hither to come; of kinsmen's approval,
Word-leave of warriors, I ween[11] that ye surely
Nothing have known. Never a greater one
Of earls o'er the earth have I had a sight of
Than is one of your number, a hero in armor;
No low-ranking fellow adorned with his weapons,
But launching them little, unless looks are deceiving,
And striking appearance. Ere ye pass on your journey

10   Edges.
11   Suppose, imagine.

As treacherous spies to the land of the Scyldings
And farther fare, I fully must know now
What race ye belong to. Ye faraway dwellers,
Sea-faring sailors, my simple opinion
Hear ye and hearken: haste is most fitting
Plainly to tell me what place ye are come from."

FIVE

The Geats Reach Heorot

THE CHIEF OF THE strangers rendered him answer,
War-troopers' leader, and word-treasure opened:
"We are sprung from the lineage of the people of Geatland,
And Higelac's hearth-friends. To heroes unnumbered
My father was known, a noble head-warrior
Ecgtheow titled; many a winter
He lived with the people, ere he passed on his journey,
Old from his dwelling; each of the counsellors
Widely mid world-folk well remembers him.
We, kindly of spirit, the lord of thy people,
The son of King Healfdene, have come here to visit,
Folk-troop's defender: be free in thy counsels!
To the noble one bear we a weighty commission,
The helm of the Danemen; we shall hide, I ween,
Naught of our message. Thou know'st if it happen,
As we soothly heard say, that some savage despoiler,
Some hidden pursuer, on nights that are murky
By deeds very direful 'mid the Danemen exhibits
Hatred unheard of, horrid destruction
And the falling of dead. From feelings least selfish
I am able to render counsel to Hrothgar,
How he, wise and worthy, may worst the destroyer,
If the anguish of sorrow should ever be lessened,
Comfort come to him, and care-waves grow cooler,
Or ever hereafter he agony suffer
And troublous distress, while towereth upward
The handsomest of houses high on the summit."

Bestriding his stallion, the strand-watchman answered,
The doughty retainer: "The difference surely
'Twixt words and works, the warlike shield-bearer
Who judgeth wisely well shall determine.
This band, I hear, beareth no malice
To the prince of the Scyldings. Pass ye then onward
With weapons and armor. I shall lead you in person;
To my war-trusty vassals command I shall issue
To keep from all injury your excellent vessel,
Your fresh-tarred craft, 'gainst every opposer
Close by the sea-shore, till the curved-neckèd bark shall
Waft back again the well-beloved hero
O'er the way of the water to Weder dominions.
To warrior so great 'twill be granted sure
In the storm of strife to stand secure."
Onward they fared then (the vessel lay quiet,
The broad-bosomed bark was bound by its cable,
Firmly at anchor); the boar-signs glistened
Bright on the visors vivid with gilding,
Blaze-hardened, brilliant; the boar acted warden.
The heroes hastened, hurried the liegemen,
Descended together, till they saw the great palace,
The well-fashioned wassail-hall wondrous and gleaming:
'Mid world-folk and kindreds that was widest reputed
Of halls under heaven which the hero abode in;
Its lustre enlightened lands without number.
Then the battle-brave hero showed them the glittering
Court of the bold ones, that they easily thither
Might fare on their journey; the aforementioned warrior
Turning his courser, quoth as he left them:
"'Tis time I were faring; Father Almighty
Grant you His grace, and give you to journey
Safe on your mission! To the sea I will get me
'Gainst hostile warriors as warden to stand."

SIX

Beowulf Introduces Himself
at the Palace

THE HIGHWAY GLISTENED with many-hued pebble,
A by-path led the liegemen together.
Firm and hand-locked the war-burnie glistened,
The ring-sword radiant rang 'mid the armor
As the party was approaching the palace together
In warlike equipments. 'Gainst the wall of the building
Their wide-fashioned war-shields they weary did set then,
Battle-shields sturdy; benchward they turned then;
Their battle-sarks[12] rattled, the gear of the heroes;
The lances stood up then, all in a cluster,
The arms of the seamen, ashen-shafts mounted
With edges of iron: the armor-clad troopers
Were decked with weapons. Then a proud-mooded hero
Asked of the champions questions of lineage:
"From what borders bear ye your battle-shields plated,
Gilded and gleaming, your gray-colored burnies,
Helmets with visors and heap of war-lances? –
To Hrothgar the king I am servant and liegeman.
'Mong folk from far-lands found I have never
Men so many of mien more courageous.
I ween that from valor, nowise as outlaws,
But from greatness of soul ye sought for King Hrothgar."
Then the strength-famous earlman answer rendered,

12   Armour.

The proud-mooded Wederchief replied to his question,
Hardy 'neath helmet: "Higelac's mates are we;
Beowulf hight I. To the bairn of Healfdene,
The famous folk-leader, I freely will tell
To thy prince my commission, if pleasantly hearing
He'll grant we may greet him so gracious to all men."
Wulfgar replied then (he was prince of the Wendels,
His boldness of spirit was known unto many,
His prowess and prudence): "The prince of the Scyldings,
The friend-lord of Danemen, I will ask of thy journey,
The giver of rings, as thou urgest me do it,
The folk-chief famous, and inform thee early
What answer the good one mindeth to render me."
He turned then hurriedly where Hrothgar was sitting,
Old and hoary, his earlmen attending him;
The strength-famous went till he stood at the shoulder
Of the lord of the Danemen, of courteous thanemen
The custom he minded. Wulfgar addressed then
His friendly liegelord: "Folk of the Geatmen
O'er the way of the waters are wafted hither,
Faring from far-lands: the foremost in rank
The battle-champions Beowulf title.
They make this petition: with thee, O my chieftain,
To be granted a conference; O gracious King Hrothgar,
Friendly answer refuse not to give them!
In war-trappings weeded[13] worthy they seem
Of earls to be honored; sure the atheling is doughty
Who headed the heroes hitherward coming."

13   Clad.

SEVEN

Hrothgar and Beowulf

HROTHGAR ANSWERED, helm of the Scyldings:
"I remember this man as the merest of striplings.
His father long dead now was Ecgtheow titled,
Him Hrethel the Geatman granted at home his
One only daughter; his battle-brave son
Is come but now, sought a trustworthy friend.
Sea-faring sailors asserted it then,
Who valuable gift-gems of the Geatmen carried
As peace-offering thither, that he thirty men's grapple
Has in his hand, the hero-in-battle.
The holy Creator usward sent him,
To West-Dane warriors, I ween, for to render
'Gainst Grendel's grimness gracious assistance:
I shall give to the good one gift-gems for courage.
Hasten to bid them hither to speed them,
To see assembled this circle of kinsmen;
Tell them expressly they're welcome in sooth to
The men of the Danes." To the door of the building
Wulfgar went then, this word-message shouted:
"My victorious liegelord bade me to tell you,
The East-Danes' atheling, that your origin knows he,
And o'er wave-billows wafted ye welcome are hither,
Valiant of spirit. Ye straightway may enter
Clad in corslets, cased in your helmets,
To see King Hrothgar. Here let your battle-boards,
Wood-spears and war-shafts, await your conferring."
The mighty one rose then, with many a liegeman,

An excellent thane-group; some there did await them,
And as bid of the brave one the battle-gear guarded.
Together they hied them, while the hero did guide them,
'Neath Heorot's roof; the high-minded went then
Sturdy 'neath helmet till he stood in the building.
Beowulf spake (his burnie did glisten,
His armor seamed over by the art of the craftsman):
"Hail thou, Hrothgar! I am Higelac's kinsman
And vassal forsooth; many a wonder
I dared as a stripling. The doings of Grendel,
In far-off fatherland I fully did know of:
Sea-farers tell us, this hall-building standeth,
Excellent edifice, empty and useless
To all the earlmen after evenlight's glimmer
'Neath heaven's bright hues hath hidden its glory.
This my earls then urged me, the most excellent of them,
Carles very clever, to come and assist thee,
Folk-leader Hrothgar; fully they knew of
The strength of my body. Themselves they beheld me
When I came from the contest, when covered with gore
Foes I escaped from, where five I had bound,
The giant-race wasted, in the waters destroying
The nickers[14] by night, bore numberless sorrows,
The Weders avenged (woes had they suffered)
Enemies ravaged; alone now with Grendel
I shall manage the matter, with the monster of evil,
The giant, decide it. Thee I would therefore
Beg of thy bounty, Bright-Danish chieftain,
Lord of the Scyldings, this single petition:
Not to refuse me, defender of warriors,
Friend-lord of folks, so far have I sought thee,
That *I* may unaided, my earlmen assisting me,
This brave-mooded war-band, purify Heorot.
I have heard on inquiry, the horrible creature
From veriest rashness recks not for weapons;
I this do scorn then, so be Higelac gracious,
My liegelord belovèd, lenient of spirit,
To bear a blade or a broad-fashioned target,
A shield to the onset; only with hand-grip

14   Sea beasts.

The foe I must grapple, fight for my life then,
Foeman with foeman; he fain must rely on
The doom of the Lord whom death layeth hold of.
I ween he will wish, if he win in the struggle,
To eat in the war-hall earls of the Geat-folk,
Boldly to swallow them, as of yore he did often
The best of the Hrethmen! Thou needest not trouble
A head-watch to give me; he will have me dripping
And dreary with gore, if death overtake me,
Will bear me off bleeding, biting and mouthing me,
The hermit will eat me, heedless of pity,
Marking the moor-fens; no more wilt thou need then
Find me my food. If I fall in the battle,
Send to Higelac the armor that serveth
To shield my bosom, the best of equipments,
Richest of ring-mails; 'tis the relic of Hrethla,
The work of Wayland. Goes Weird as she must go!"

EIGHT

Hrothgar and Beowulf – Continued

HROTHGAR DISCOURSED, helm of the Scyldings:
"To defend our folk and to furnish assistance,
Thou soughtest us hither, good friend Beowulf.
The fiercest of feuds thy father engaged in,
Heatholaf killed he in hand-to-hand conflict
'Mid Wilfingish warriors; then the Wederish people
For fear of a feud were forced to disown him.
Thence flying he fled to the folk of the South-Danes,
The race of the Scyldings, o'er the roll of the waters;
I had lately begun then to govern the Danemen,
The hoard-seat of heroes held in my youth,
Rich in its jewels: dead was Heregar,
My kinsman and elder had earth-joys forsaken,
Healfdene his bairn. He was better than I am!
That feud thereafter for a fee I compounded;
O'er the weltering waters to the Wilfings I sent
Ornaments old; oaths did he swear me.
It pains me in spirit to any to tell it,
What grief in Heorot Grendel hath caused me,
What horror unlooked-for, by hatred unceasing.
Waned is my war-band, wasted my hall-troop;
Weird hath offcast them to the clutches of Grendel.
God can easily hinder the scather
From deeds so direful. Oft drunken with beer
O'er the ale-vessel promised warriors in armor
They would willingly wait on the wassailing-benches
A grapple with Grendel, with grimmest of edges.

Then this mead-hall at morning with murder was reeking,
The building was bloody at breaking of daylight,
The bench-deals all flooded, dripping and bloodied,
The folk-hall was gory: I had fewer retainers,
Dear-beloved warriors, whom death had laid hold of.
Sit at the feast now, thy intents unto heroes,
Thy victor-fame show, as thy spirit doth urge thee!"
For the men of the Geats then together assembled,
In the beer-hall blithesome a bench was made ready;
There warlike in spirit they went to be seated,
Proud and exultant. A liegeman did service,
Who a beaker embellished bore with decorum,
And gleaming-drink poured. The gleeman sang whilom[15]
Hearty in Heorot; there was heroes' rejoicing,
A numerous war-band of Weders and Danemen.

---

15   At times, formerly, often.

NINE

Unferth Taunts Beowulf

UNFERTH SPOKE UP, Ecglaf his son,
Who sat at the feet of the lord of the Scyldings,
Opened the jousting (the journey of Beowulf,
Sea-farer doughty, gave sorrow to Unferth
And greatest chagrin, too, for granted he never
That any man else on earth should attain to,
Gain under heaven, more glory than he):
"Art thou that Beowulf with Breca did struggle,
On the wide sea-currents at swimming contended,
Where to humor your pride the ocean ye tried,
From vainest vaunting adventured your bodies
In care of the waters? And no one was able
Nor lief nor loth one, in the least to dissuade you
Your difficult voyage; then ye ventured a-swimming,
Where your arms outstretching the streams ye did cover,
The mere-ways[16] measured, mixing and stirring them,
Glided the ocean; angry the waves were,
With the weltering of winter. In the water's possession,
Ye toiled for a seven-night; he at swimming outdid thee,
In strength excelled thee. Then early at morning
On the Heathoremes' shore the holm-currents tossed him,
Sought he thenceward the home of his fathers,
Beloved of his liegemen, the land of the Brondings,
The peace-castle pleasant, where a people he wielded,
Had borough and jewels. The pledge that he made thee

---

16   Sea; in compounds, "mere-ways," "mere-currents," etc.

The son of Beanstan hath soothly accomplished.
Then I ween thou wilt find thee less fortunate issue,
Though ever triumphant in onset of battle,
A grim grappling, if Grendel thou darest
For the space of a night near-by to wait for!"
Beowulf answered, offspring of Ecgtheow:
"My good friend Unferth, sure freely and wildly,
Thou fuddled with beer of Breca hast spoken,
Hast told of his journey! A fact I allege it,
That greater strength in the waters I had then,
Ills in the ocean, than any man else had.
We made agreement as the merest of striplings
Promised each other (both of us then were
Younkers in years) that we yet would adventure
Out on the ocean; it all we accomplished.
While swimming the sea-floods, sword-blade unscabbarded
Boldly we brandished, our bodies expected
To shield from the sharks. He sure was unable
To swim on the waters further than I could,
More swift on the waves, nor *would* I from him go.
Then we two companions stayed in the ocean
Five nights together, till the currents did part us,
The weltering waters, weathers the bleakest,
And nethermost night, and the north-wind whistled
Fierce in our faces; fell were the billows.
The mere fishes' mood was mightily ruffled:
And there against foemen my firm-knotted corslet,
Hand-jointed, hardy, help did afford me;
My battle-sark braided, brilliantly gilded,
Lay on my bosom. To the bottom then dragged me,
A hateful fiend-scather, seized me and held me,
Grim in his grapple: 'twas granted me, nathless,
To pierce the monster with the point of my weapon,
My obedient blade; battle offcarried
The mighty mere-creature by means of my hand-blow.

TEN

Beowulf Silences Unferth – Glee is High

"SO ILL-MEANING ENEMIES often did cause me
Sorrow the sorest. I served them, in quittance,
With my dear-lovèd sword, as in sooth it was fitting;
They missed the pleasure of feasting abundantly,
Ill-doers evil, of eating my body,
Of surrounding the banquet deep in the ocean;
But wounded with edges early at morning
They were stretched a-high on the strand of the ocean,
Put to sleep with the sword, that sea-going travelers
No longer thereafter were hindered from sailing
The foam-dashing currents. Came a light from the east,
God's beautiful beacon; the billows subsided,
That well I could see the nesses projecting,
The blustering crags. Weird often saveth
The undoomed hero if doughty his valor!
But me did it fortune to fell with my weapon
Nine of the nickers. Of night-struggle harder
'Neath dome of the heaven heard I but rarely,
Nor of wight[17] more woeful in the waves of the ocean;
Yet I 'scaped with my life the grip of the monsters,
Weary from travel. Then the waters bare me
To the land of the Finns, the flood with the current,
The weltering waves. Not a word hath been told me

17   Creature.

Of deeds so daring done by thee, Unferth,
And of sword-terror none; never hath Breca
At the play of the battle, nor either of you two,
Feat so fearless performèd with weapons
Glinting and gleaming ⊠
⊠ I utter no boasting;
Though with cold-blooded cruelty thou killedst thy brothers,
Thy nearest of kin; thou needs must in hell get
Direful damnation, though doughty thy wisdom.
I tell thee in earnest, offspring of Ecglaf,
Never had Grendel such numberless horrors,
The direful demon, done to thy liegelord,
Harrying in Heorot, if thy heart were as sturdy,
Thy mood as ferocious as thou dost describe them.
He hath found out fully that the fierce-burning hatred,
The edge-battle eager, of all of your kindred,
Of the Victory-Scyldings, need little dismay him:
Oaths he exacteth, not any he spares
Of the folk of the Danemen, but fighteth with pleasure,
Killeth and feasteth, no contest expecteth
From Spear-Danish people. But the prowess and valor
Of the earls of the Geatmen early shall venture
To give him a grapple. He shall go who is able
Bravely to banquet, when the bright-light of morning
Which the second day bringeth, the sun in its ether-robes,
O'er children of men shines from the southward!"
Then the gray-haired, war-famed giver of treasure
Was blithesome and joyous, the Bright-Danish ruler
Expected assistance; the people's protector
Heard from Beowulf his bold resolution.
There was laughter of heroes; loud was the clatter,
The words were winsome. Wealhtheow advanced then,
Consort of Hrothgar, of courtesy mindful,
Gold-decked saluted the men in the building,
And the freeborn woman the beaker presented
To the lord of the kingdom, first of the East-Danes,
Bade him be blithesome when beer was a-flowing,
Lief to his liegemen; he lustily tasted
Of banquet and beaker, battle-famed ruler.
The Helmingish lady then graciously circled
'Mid all the liegemen lesser and greater:

Treasure-cups tendered, till time was afforded
That the decorous-mooded, diademed folk-queen
Might bear to Beowulf the bumper o'errunning;
She greeted the Geat-prince, God she did thank,
Most wise in her words, that her wish was accomplished,
That in any of earlmen she ever should look for
Solace in sorrow. He accepted the beaker,
Battle-bold warrior, at Wealhtheow's giving,
Then equipped for combat quoth he in measures,
Beowulf spake, offspring of Ecgtheow:
"I purposed in spirit when I mounted the ocean,
When I boarded my boat with a band of my liegemen,
I would work to the fullest the will of your people
Or in foe's-clutches fastened fall in the battle.
Deeds I shall do of daring and prowess,
Or the last of my life-days live in this mead-hall."
These words to the lady were welcome and pleasing,
The boast of the Geatman; with gold trappings broidered
Went the freeborn folk-queen her fond-lord to sit by.
Then again as of yore was heard in the building
Courtly discussion, conquerors' shouting,
Heroes were happy, till Healfdene's son would
Go to his slumber to seek for refreshing;
For the horrid hell-monster in the hall-building knew he
A fight was determined, since the light of the sun they
No longer could see, and lowering darkness
O'er all had descended, and dark under heaven
Shadowy shapes came shying around them.
The liegemen all rose then. One saluted the other,
Hrothgar Beowulf, in rhythmical measures,
Wishing him well, and, the wassail-hall giving
To his care and keeping, quoth he departing:
"Not to any one else have I ever entrusted,
But thee and thee only, the hall of the Danemen,
Since high I could heave my hand and my buckler.
Take thou in charge now the noblest of houses;
Be mindful of honor, exhibiting prowess,
Watch 'gainst the foeman! Thou shalt want no enjoyments,
Survive thou safely adventure so glorious!"

ELEVEN

All Sleep Save One

THEN HROTHGAR DEPARTED, his earl-throng attending him,
Folk-lord of Scyldings, forth from the building;
The war-chieftain wished then Wealhtheow to look for,
The queen for a bedmate. To keep away Grendel
The Glory of Kings[18] had given a hall-watch,
As men heard recounted: for the king of the Danemen
He did special service, gave the giant a watcher:
And the prince of the Geatmen implicitly trusted
His warlike strength and the Wielder's protection.
His armor of iron off him he did then,
His helmet from his head, to his henchman committed
His chased-handled chain-sword, choicest of weapons,
And bade him bide with his battle-equipments.
The good one then uttered words of defiance,
Beowulf Geatman, ere his bed he upmounted:
"I hold me no meaner in matters of prowess,
In warlike achievements, than Grendel does himself;
Hence I seek not with sword-edge to sooth him to slumber,
Of life to bereave him, though well I am able.
No battle-skill has he, that blows he should strike me,
To shatter my shield, though sure he is mighty
In strife and destruction; but struggling by night we
Shall do without edges, dare he to look for
Weaponless warfare, and wise-mooded Father
The glory apportion, God ever-holy,

---

18   God.

On which hand soever to him seemeth proper."
Then the brave-mooded hero bent to his slumber,
The pillow received the cheek of the noble;
And many a martial mere-thane attending
Sank to his slumber. Seemed it unlikely
That ever thereafter any should hope to
Be happy at home, hero-friends visit
Or the lordly troop-castle where he lived from his childhood;
They had heard how slaughter had snatched from the wine-hall,
Had recently ravished, of the race of the Scyldings
Too many by far. But the Lord to them granted
The weaving of war-speed,[19] to Wederish heroes
Aid and comfort, that every opponent
By one man's war-might they worsted and vanquished,
By the might of himself; the truth is established
That God Almighty hath governed for ages
Kindreds and nations. A night very lurid
The trav'ler-at-twilight came tramping and striding.
The warriors were sleeping who should watch the horned-building,
One only excepted. 'Mid earthmen 'twas 'stablished,
Th' implacable foeman was powerless to hurl them
To the land of shadows, if the Lord were unwilling;
But serving as warder, in terror to foemen,
He angrily bided the issue of battle.

19   Success in war.

TWELVE

Grendel and Beowulf

'NEATH THE CLOUDY CLIFFS came from the moor then
Grendel going, God's anger bare he.
The monster intended some one of earthmen
In the hall-building grand to entrap and make way with:
He went under welkin where well he knew of
The wine-joyous building, brilliant with plating,
Gold-hall of earthmen. Not the earliest occasion
He the home and manor of Hrothgar had sought:
Ne'er found he in life-days later nor earlier
Hardier hero, hall-thanes more sturdy!
Then came to the building the warrior marching,
Bereft of his joyance. The door quickly opened
On fire-hinges fastened, when his fingers had touched it;
The fell one had flung then – his fury so bitter –
Open the entrance. Early thereafter
The foeman trod the shining hall-pavement,
Strode he angrily; from the eyes of him glimmered
A lustre unlovely likest to fire.
He beheld in the hall the heroes in numbers,
A circle of kinsmen sleeping together,
A throng of thanemen: then his thoughts were exultant,
He minded to sunder from each of the thanemen
The life from his body, horrible demon,
Ere morning came, since fate had allowed him
The prospect of plenty. Providence willed not
To permit him any more of men under heaven
To eat in the night-time. Higelac's kinsman

Great sorrow endured how the dire-mooded creature`
In unlooked-for assaults were likely to bear him.
No thought had the monster of deferring the matter,
But on earliest occasion he quickly laid hold of
A soldier asleep, suddenly tore him,
Bit his bone-prison, the blood drank in currents,
Swallowed in mouthfuls: he soon had the dead man's
Feet and hands, too, eaten entirely.
Nearer he strode then, the stout-hearted warrior
Snatched as he slumbered, seizing with hand-grip,
Forward the foeman foined with his hand;
Caught he quickly the cunning deviser,
On his elbow he rested. This early discovered
The master of malice, that in middle-earth's regions,
'Neath the whole of the heavens, no hand-grapple greater
In any man else had he ever encountered:
Fearful in spirit, faint-mooded waxed he,
Not off could betake him; death he was pondering,
Would fly to his covert, seek the devils' assembly:
His calling no more was the same he had followed
Long in his lifetime. The liege-kinsman worthy
Of Higelac minded his speech of the evening,
Stood he up straight and stoutly did seize him.
His fingers crackled; the giant was outward,
The earl stepped farther. The famous one minded
To flee away farther, if he found an occasion,
And off and away, avoiding delay,
To fly to the fen-moors; he fully was ware of
The strength of his grapple in the grip of the foeman.
'Twas an ill-taken journey that the injury-bringing,
Harrying harmer to Heorot wandered:
The palace re-echoed; to all of the Danemen,
Dwellers in castles, to each of the bold ones,
Earlmen, was terror. Angry they both were,
Archwarders raging. Rattled the building;
'Twas a marvellous wonder that the wine-hall withstood then
The bold-in-battle, bent not to earthward,
Excellent earth-hall; but within and without it
Was fastened so firmly in fetters of iron,
By the art of the armorer. Off from the sill there
Bent mead-benches many, as men have informed me,

Adorned with gold-work, where the grim ones did struggle.
The Scylding wise men weened ne'er before
That by might and main-strength a man under heaven
Might break it in pieces, bone-decked, resplendent,
Crush it by cunning, unless clutch of the fire
In smoke should consume it. The sound mounted upward
Novel enough; on the North Danes fastened
A terror of anguish, on all of the men there
Who heard from the wall the weeping and plaining,
The song of defeat from the foeman of heaven,
Heard him hymns of horror howl, and his sorrow
Hell-bound bewailing. He held him too firmly
Who was strongest of main-strength of men of that era.

THIRTEEN

Grendel Is Vanquished

FOR NO CAUSE WHATEVER would the earlmen's defender
Leave in life-joys the loathsome newcomer,
He deemed his existence utterly useless
To men under heaven. Many a noble
Of Beowulf brandished his battle-sword old,
Would guard the life of his lord and protector,
The far-famed chieftain, if able to do so;
While waging the warfare, this wist they but little,
Brave battle-thanes, while his body intending
To slit into slivers, and seeking his spirit:
That the relentless foeman nor finest of weapons
Of all on the earth, nor any of war-bills
Was willing to injure; but weapons of victory
Swords and suchlike he had sworn to dispense with.
His death at that time must prove to be wretched,
And the faraway spirit widely should journey
Into enemies' power. This plainly he saw then
Who with mirth of mood malice no little
Had wrought in the past on the race of the earthmen
(To God he was hostile), that his body would fail him,
But Higelac's hardy henchman and kinsman
Held him by the hand; hateful to other
Was each one if living. A body-wound suffered
The direful demon, damage incurable
Was seen on his shoulder, his sinews were shivered,
His body did burst. To Beowulf was given
Glory in battle; Grendel from thenceward

Must flee and hide him in the fen-cliffs and marshes,
Sick unto death, his dwelling must look for
Unwinsome and woeful; he wist the more fully
The end of his earthly existence was nearing,
His life-days' limits. At last for the Danemen,
When the slaughter was over, their wish was accomplished.
The comer-from-far-land had cleansed then of evil,
Wise and valiant, the war-hall of Hrothgar,
Saved it from violence. He joyed in the night-work,
In repute for prowess; the prince of the Geatmen
For the East-Danish people his boast had accomplished,
Bettered their burdensome bale-sorrows fully,
The craft-begot evil they erstwhile had suffered
And were forced to endure from crushing oppression,
Their manifold misery. 'Twas a manifest token,
When the hero-in-battle the hand suspended,
The arm and the shoulder (there was all of the claw
Of Grendel together) 'neath great-stretching hall-roof.

FOURTEEN

Rejoicing of the Danes

IN THE MIST OF THE morning many a warrior
Stood round the gift-hall, as the story is told me:
Folk-princes fared then from far and from near
Through long-stretching journeys to look at the wonder,
The footprints of the foeman. Few of the warriors
Who gazed on the foot-tracks of the inglorious creature
His parting from life pained very deeply,
How, weary in spirit, off from those regions
In combats conquered he carried his traces,
Fated and flying, to the flood of the nickers.
There in bloody billows bubbled the currents,
The angry eddy was everywhere mingled
And seething with gore, welling with sword-blood;
He death-doomed had hid him, when reaved of his joyance
He laid down his life in the lair he had fled to,
His heathenish spirit, where hell did receive him.
Thence the friends from of old backward turned them,
And many a younker from merry adventure,
Striding their stallions, stout from the seaward,
Heroes on horses. There were heard very often
Beowulf's praises; many often asserted
That neither south nor north, in the circuit of waters,
O'er outstretching earth-plain, none other was better
'Mid bearers of war-shields, more worthy to govern,
'Neath the arch of the ether. Not any, however,
'Gainst the friend-lord muttered, mocking-words uttered
Of Hrothgar the gracious (a good king he).

Oft the famed ones permitted their fallow-skinned horses
To run in rivalry, racing and chasing,
Where the fieldways appeared to them fair and inviting,
Known for their excellence; oft a thane of the folk-lord,
A man of celebrity, mindful of rhythms,
Who ancient traditions treasured in memory,
New word-groups found properly bound:
The bard after 'gan then Beowulf's venture
Wisely to tell of, and words that were clever
To utter skilfully, earnestly speaking,
Everything told he that he heard as to Sigmund's
Mighty achievements, many things hidden,
The strife of the Waelsing, the wide-going ventures
The children of men knew of but little,
The feud and the fury, but Fitela with him,
When suchlike matters he minded to speak of,
Uncle to nephew, as in every contention
Each to other was ever devoted:
A numerous host of the race of the scathers
They had slain with the sword-edge. To Sigmund accrued then
No little of glory, when his life-days were over,
Since he sturdy in struggle had destroyed the great dragon,
The hoard-treasure's keeper; 'neath the hoar-grayish stone he,
The son of the atheling, unaided adventured
The perilous project; not present was Fitela,
Yet the fortune befell him of forcing his weapon
Through the marvellous dragon, that it stood in the wall,
Well-honored weapon; the worm was slaughtered.
The great one had gained then by his glorious achievement
To reap from the ring-hoard richest enjoyment,
As best it did please him: his vessel he loaded,
Shining ornaments on the ship's bosom carried,
Kinsman of Waels: the drake in heat melted.
He was farthest famed of fugitive pilgrims,
Mid wide-scattered world-folk, for works of great prowess,
War-troopers' shelter: hence waxed he in honor.
Afterward Heremod's hero-strength failed him,
His vigor and valor. 'Mid venomous haters
To the hands of foemen he was foully delivered,
Offdriven early. Agony-billows
Oppressed him too long, to his people he became then,

To all the athelings, an ever-great burden;
And the daring one's journey in days of yore
Many wise men were wont to deplore,
Such as hoped he would bring them help in their sorrow,
That the son of their ruler should rise into power,
Holding the headship held by his fathers,
Should govern the people, the gold-hoard and borough,
The kingdom of heroes, the realm of the Scyldings.
He to all men became then far more beloved,
Higelac's kinsman, to kindreds and races,
To his friends much dearer; him malice assaulted. –
Oft running and racing on roadsters they measured
The dun-colored highways. Then the light of the morning
Was hurried and hastened. Went henchmen in numbers
To the beautiful building, bold ones in spirit,
To look at the wonder; the liegelord himself then
From his wife-bower wending, warden of treasures,
Glorious trod with troopers unnumbered,
Famed for his virtues, and with him the queen-wife
Measured the mead-ways, with maidens attending.

FIFTEEN

Hrothgar's Gratitude

HROTHGAR DISCOURSED (to the hall-building went he,
He stood by the pillar, saw the steep-rising hall-roof
Gleaming with gold-gems, and Grendel his hand there):
"For the sight we behold now, thanks to the Wielder
Early be offered! Much evil I bided,
Snaring from Grendel: God can e'er 'complish
Wonder on wonder, Wielder of Glory!
But lately I reckoned ne'er under heaven
Comfort to gain me for any of sorrows,
While the handsomest of houses horrid with bloodstain
Gory uptowered; grief had offfrightened
Each of the wise ones who weened not that ever
The folk-troop's defences 'gainst foes they should strengthen,
'Gainst sprites and monsters. Through the might of the Wielder
A doughty retainer hath a deed now accomplished
Which erstwhile we all with our excellent wisdom
Failed to perform. May affirm very truly
What woman soever in all of the nations
Gave birth to the child, if yet she surviveth,
That the long-ruling Lord was lavish to herward
In the birth of the bairn. Now, Beowulf dear,
Most excellent hero, I'll love thee in spirit
As bairn of my body; bear well henceforward
The relationship new. No lack shall befall thee
Of earth-joys any I ever can give thee.
Full often for lesser service I've given
Hero less hardy hoard-treasure precious,

To a weaker in war-strife. By works of distinction
Thou hast gained for thyself now that thy glory shall flourish
Forever and ever. The All-Ruler quite[20] thee
With good from His hand as He hitherto did thee!"
Beowulf answered, Ecgtheow's offspring:
"That labor of glory most gladly achieved we,
The combat accomplished, unquailing we ventured
The enemy's grapple; I would grant it much rather
Thou wert able to look at the creature in person,
Faint unto falling, the foe in his trappings!
On murder-bed quickly I minded to bind him,
With firm-holding fetters, that forced by my grapple
Low he should lie in life-and-death struggle
'Less his body escape; I was wholly unable,
Since God did not will it, to keep him from going,
Not held him that firmly, hated opposer;
Too swift was the foeman. Yet safety regarding
He suffered his hand behind him to linger,
His arm and shoulder, to act as watcher;
No shadow of solace the woe-begone creature
Found him there nathless: the hated destroyer
Liveth no longer, lashed for his evils,
But sorrow hath seized him, in snare-meshes hath him
Close in its clutches, keepeth him writhing
In baleful bonds: there banished for evil
The man shall wait for the mighty tribunal,
How the God of glory shall give him his earnings."
Then the soldier kept silent, son of old Ecglaf,
From boasting and bragging of battle-achievements,
Since the princes beheld there the hand that depended
'Neath the lofty hall-timbers by the might of the nobleman,
Each one before him, the enemy's fingers;
Each finger-nail strong steel most resembled,
The heathen one's hand-spur, the hero-in-battle's
Claw most uncanny;[21] quoth they agreeing,
That not any excellent edges of brave ones
Was willing to touch him, the terrible creature's
Battle-hand bloody to bear away from him.

20   Requite.
21   Ill-featured, grizzly.

SIXTEEN

Hrothgar Lavishes Gifts Upon His Deliverer

THEN STRAIGHT WAS ORDERED that Heorot inside
With hands be embellished: a host of them gathered,
Of men and women, who the wassailing-building
The guest-hall begeared.[22] Gold-flashing sparkled
Webs[23] on the walls then, of wonders a many
To each of the heroes that look on such objects.
The beautiful building was broken to pieces
Which all within with irons was fastened,
Its hinges torn off: only the roof was
Whole and uninjured when the horrible creature
Outlawed for evil off had betaken him,
Hopeless of living. 'Tis hard to avoid it
(Whoever will do it!); but he doubtless must come to
The place awaiting, as Wyrd hath appointed,
Soul-bearers, earth-dwellers, earls under heaven,
Where bound on its bed his body shall slumber
When feasting is finished. Full was the time then
That the son of Healfdene went to the building;
The excellent atheling would eat of the banquet.
Ne'er heard I that people with hero-band larger
Bare them better tow'rds their bracelet-bestower.
The laden-with-glory stooped to the bench then

22   Prepared.
23   Tapestries.

(Their kinsmen-companions in plenty were joyful,
Many a cupful quaffing complaisantly),
Doughty of spirit in the high-tow'ring palace,
Hrothgar and Hrothulf. Heorot then inside
Was filled with friendly ones; falsehood and treachery
The Folk-Scyldings now nowise did practise.
Then the offspring of Healfdene offered to Beowulf
A golden standard, as reward for the victory,
A banner embossed, burnie and helmet;
Many men saw then a song-famous weapon
Borne 'fore the hero. Beowulf drank of
The cup in the building; that treasure-bestowing
He needed not blush for in battle-men's presence.
Ne'er heard I that many men on the ale-bench
In friendlier fashion to their fellows presented
Four bright jewels with gold-work embellished.
'Round the roof of the helmet a head-guarder outside
Braided with wires, with bosses was furnished,
That swords-for-the-battle fight-hardened might fail
Boldly to harm him, when the hero proceeded
Forth against foemen. The defender of earls then
Commanded that eight steeds with bridles
Gold-plated, gleaming, be guided to hallward,
Inside the building; on one of them stood then
An art-broidered saddle embellished with jewels;
'Twas the sovereign's seat, when the son of King Healfdene
Was pleased to take part in the play of the edges;
The famous one's valor ne'er failed at the front when
Slain ones were bowing. And to Beowulf granted
The prince of the Ingwins, power over both,
O'er war-steeds and weapons; bade him well to enjoy them.
In so manly a manner the mighty-famed chieftain,
Hoard-ward of heroes, with horses and jewels
War-storms requited, that none e'er condemneth
Who willeth to tell truth with full justice.

SEVENTEEN

Banquet (Continued) – The Scop's Song of Finn and Hnaef

AND THE ATHELING OF earlmen to each of the heroes
Who the ways of the waters went with Beowulf,
A costly gift-token gave on the mead-bench,
Offered an heirloom, and ordered that that man
With gold should be paid for, whom Grendel had erstwhile
Wickedly slaughtered, as he more of them had done
Had far-seeing God and the mood of the hero
The fate not averted: the Father then governed
All of the earth-dwellers, as He ever is doing;
Hence insight for all men is everywhere fittest,
Forethought of spirit! much he shall suffer
Of lief and of loathsome who long in this present
Useth the world in this woeful existence.
There was music and merriment mingling together
Touching Healfdene's leader; the joy-wood was fingered,
Measures recited, when the singer of Hrothgar
On mead-bench should mention the merry hall-joyance
Of the kinsmen of Finn, when onset surprised them:
"The Half-Danish hero, Hnaef of the Scyldings,
On the field of the Frisians was fated to perish.
Sure Hildeburg needed not mention approving
The faith of the Jutemen: though blameless entirely,
When shields were shivered she was shorn of her darlings,
Of bairns and brothers: they bent to their fate
With war-spear wounded; woe was that woman.

Not causeless lamented the daughter of Hoce
The decree of the Wielder when morning-light came and
She was able 'neath heaven to behold the destruction
Of brothers and bairns, where the brightest of earth-joys
She had hitherto had: all the henchmen of Finn
War had offtaken, save a handful remaining,
That he nowise was able to offer resistance
To the onset of Hengest in the parley of battle,
Nor the wretched remnant to rescue in war from
The earl of the atheling; but they offered conditions,
Another great building to fully make ready,
A hall and a high-seat, that half they might rule with
The sons of the Jutemen, and that Folcwalda's son would
Day after day the Danemen honor
When gifts were giving, and grant of his ring-store
To Hengest's earl-troop ever so freely,
Of his gold-plated jewels, as he encouraged the Frisians
On the bench of the beer-hall. On both sides they swore then
A fast-binding compact; Finn unto Hengest
With no thought of revoking vowed then most solemnly
The woe-begone remnant well to take charge of,
His Witan advising; the agreement should no one
By words or works weaken and shatter,
By artifice ever injure its value,
Though reaved of their ruler their ring-giver's slayer
They followed as vassals, Fate so requiring:
Then if one of the Frisians the quarrel should speak of
In tones that were taunting, terrible edges
Should cut in requital. Accomplished the oath was,
And treasure of gold from the hoard was uplifted.
The best of the Scylding braves was then fully
Prepared for the pile; at the pyre was seen clearly
The blood-gory burnie, the boar with his gilding,
The iron-hard swine, athelings many
Fatally wounded; no few had been slaughtered.
Hildeburg bade then, at the burning of Hnaef,
The bairn of her bosom to bear to the fire,
That his body be burned and borne to the pyre.
The woe-stricken woman wept on his shoulder
In measures lamented; upmounted the hero.
The greatest of dead-fires curled to the welkin,

On the hill's-front crackled; heads were a-melting,
Wound-doors bursting, while the blood was a-coursing
From body-bite fierce. The fire devoured them,
Greediest of spirits, whom war had offcarried
From both of the peoples; their bravest were fallen.

EIGHTEEN

The Finn Episode (Continued) – The Banquet Continues

"THEN THE WARRIORS departed to go to their dwellings,
Reaved of their friends, Friesland to visit,
Their homes and high-city. Hengest continued
Biding with Finn the blood-tainted winter,
Wholly unsundered; of fatherland thought he
Though unable to drive the ring-stemmèd vessel
O'er the ways of the waters; the wave-deeps were tossing,
Fought with the wind; winter in ice-bonds
Closed up the currents, till there came to the dwelling
A year in its course, as yet it revolveth,
If season propitious one alway regardeth,
World-cheering weathers. Then winter was gone,
Earth's bosom was lovely; the exile would get him,
The guest from the palace; on gruesomest vengeance
He brooded more eager than on oversea journeys,
Whe'r onset-of-anger he were able to 'complish,
The bairns of the Jutemen therein to remember.
Nowise refused he the duties of liegeman
When Hun of the Frisians the battle-sword Láfing,
Fairest of falchions, friendly did give him:
Its edges were famous in folk-talk of Jutland.
And savage sword-fury seized in its clutches
Bold-mooded Finn where he bode in his palace,
When the gruesome grapple Guthlaf and Oslaf

Had mournfully mentioned, the mere-journey over,
For sorrows half-blamed him; the flickering spirit
Could not bide in his bosom. Then the building was covered
With corpses of foemen, and Finn too was slaughtered,
The king with his comrades, and the queen made a prisoner.
The troops of the Scyldings bore to their vessels
All that the land-king had in his palace,
Such trinkets and treasures they took as, on searching,
At Finn's they could find. They ferried to Daneland
The excellent woman on oversea journey,
Led her to their land-folk." The lay was concluded,
The gleeman's recital. Shouts again rose then,
Bench-glee resounded, bearers then offered
Wine from wonder-vats. Wealhtheo advanced then
Going 'neath gold-crown, where the good ones were seated
Uncle and nephew; their peace was yet mutual,
True each to the other. And Unferth the spokesman
Sat at the feet of the lord of the Scyldings:
Each trusted his spirit that his mood was courageous,
Though at fight he had failed in faith to his kinsmen.
Said the queen of the Scyldings: "My lord and protector,
Treasure-bestower, take thou this beaker;
Joyance attend thee, gold-friend of heroes,
And greet thou the Geatmen with gracious responses!
So ought one to do. Be kind to the Geatmen,
In gifts not niggardly; anear and afar now
Peace thou enjoyest. Report hath informed me
Thou'lt have for a bairn the battle-brave hero.
Now is Heorot cleansèd, ring-palace gleaming;
Give while thou mayest many rewards,
And bequeath to thy kinsmen kingdom and people,
On wending thy way to the Wielder's splendor.
I know good Hrothulf, that the noble young troopers
He'll care for and honor, lord of the Scyldings,
If earth-joys thou endest earlier than he doth;
I reckon that recompense he'll render with kindness
Our offspring and issue, if that all he remember,
What favors of yore, when he yet was an infant,
We awarded to him for his worship and pleasure."
Then she turned by the bench where her sons were carousing,

Hrethric and Hrothmund, and the heroes' offspring,
The war-youth together; there the good one was sitting
'Twixt the brothers twain, Beowulf Geatman.

NINETEEN

Beowulf Receives Further Honor

A BEAKER WAS BORNE HIM, and bidding to quaff it
Graciously given, and gold that was twisted
Pleasantly proffered, a pair of arm-jewels,
Rings and corslet, of collars the greatest
I've heard of 'neath heaven. Of heroes not any
More splendid from jewels have I heard 'neath the welkin,
Since Hama off bore the Brosingmen's necklace,
The bracteates[24] and jewels, from the bright-shining city,
Eormenric's cunning craftiness fled from,
Chose gain everlasting. Geatish Higelac,
Grandson of Swerting, last had this jewel
When tramping 'neath banner the treasure he guarded,
The field-spoil defended; Fate offcarried him
When for deeds of daring he endured tribulation,
Hate from the Frisians; the ornaments bare he
O'er the cup of the currents, costly gem-treasures,
Mighty folk-leader, he fell 'neath his target;
The corpse of the king then came into charge of
The race of the Frankmen, the mail-shirt and collar:
Warmen less noble plundered the fallen,
When the fight was finished; the folk of the Geatmen
The field of the dead held in possession.
The choicest of mead-halls with cheering resounded.
Wealhtheo discoursed, the war-troop addressed she:
"This collar enjoy thou, Beowulf worthy,

24   Necklaces with round ornaments.

Young man, in safety, and use thou this armor,
Gems of the people, and prosper thou fully,
Show thyself sturdy and be to these liegemen
Mild with instruction! I'll mind thy requital.
Thou hast brought it to pass that far and near
Forever and ever earthmen shall honor thee,
Even so widely as ocean surroundeth
The blustering bluffs. Be, while thou livest,
A wealth-blessèd atheling. I wish thee most truly
Jewels and treasure. Be kind to my son, thou
Living in joyance! Here each of the nobles
Is true unto other, gentle in spirit,
Loyal to leader. The liegemen are peaceful,
The war-troops ready: well-drunken heroes,
Do as I bid ye." Then she went to the settle.
There was choicest of banquets, wine drank the heroes:
Weird they knew not, destiny cruel,
As to many an earlman early it happened,
When evening had come and Hrothgar had parted
Off to his manor, the mighty to slumber.
Warriors unnumbered warded the building
As erst they did often: the ale-settle bared they,
'Twas covered all over with beds and pillows.
Doomed unto death, down to his slumber
Bowed then a beer-thane. Their battle-shields placed they,
Bright-shining targets, up by their heads then;
O'er the atheling on ale-bench 'twas easy to see there
Battle-high helmet, burnie of ring-mail,
And mighty war-spear. 'Twas the wont of that people
To constantly keep them equipped for the battle,
At home or marching – in either condition –
At seasons just such as necessity ordered
As best for their ruler; that people was worthy.

TWENTY

The Mother of Grendel

THEY SANK THEN TO SLUMBER. With sorrow one paid for
His evening repose, as often betid them
While Grendel was holding the gold-bedecked palace,
Ill-deeds performing, till his end overtook him,
Death for his sins. 'Twas seen very clearly,
Known unto earth-folk, that still an avenger
Outlived the loathed one, long since the sorrow
Caused by the struggle; the mother of Grendel,
Devil-shaped woman, her woe ever minded,
Who was held to inhabit the horrible waters,
The cold-flowing currents, after Cain had become a
Slayer-with-edges to his one only brother,
The son of his sire; he set out then banished,
Marked as a murderer, man-joys avoiding,
Lived in the desert. Thence demons unnumbered
Fate-sent awoke; one of them Grendel,
Sword-cursèd, hateful, who at Heorot met with
A man that was watching, waiting the struggle,
Where a horrid one held him with hand-grapple sturdy;
Nathless he minded the might of his body,
The glorious gift God had allowed him,
And folk-ruling Father's favor relied on,
His help and His comfort: so he conquered the foeman,
The hell-spirit humbled: he unhappy departed then,
Reaved of his joyance, journeying to death-haunts,
Foeman of man. His mother moreover
Eager and gloomy was anxious to go on

Her mournful mission, mindful of vengeance
For the death of her son. She came then to Heorot
Where the Armor-Dane earlmen all through the building
Were lying in slumber. Soon there became then
Return to the nobles, when the mother of Grendel
Entered the folk-hall; the fear was less grievous
By even so much as the vigor of maidens,
War-strength of women, by warrior is reckoned,
When well-carved weapon, worked with the hammer,
Blade very bloody, brave with its edges,
Strikes down the boar-sign that stands on the helmet.
Then the hard-edgèd weapon was heaved in the building,
The brand[25] o'er the benches, broad-lindens many
Hand-fast were lifted; for helmet he recked not,
For armor-net broad, whom terror laid hold of.
She went then hastily, outward would get her
Her life for to save, when some one did spy her;
Soon she had grappled one of the athelings
Fast and firmly, when fenward she hied her;
That one to Hrothgar was liefest of heroes
In rank of retainer where waters encircle,
A mighty shield-warrior, whom she murdered at slumber,
A broadly-famed battle-knight. Beowulf was absent,
But another apartment was erstwhile devoted
To the glory-decked Geatman when gold was distributed.
There was hubbub in Heorot. The hand that was famous
She grasped in its gore; grief was renewed then
In homes and houses: 'twas no happy arrangement
In both of the quarters to barter and purchase
With lives of their friends. Then the well-agèd ruler,
The gray-headed war-thane, was woeful in spirit,
When his long-trusted liegeman lifeless he knew of,
His dearest one gone. Quick from a room was
Beowulf brought, brave and triumphant.
As day was dawning in the dusk of the morning,
Went then that earlman, champion noble,
Came with comrades, where the clever one bided
Whether God all gracious would grant him a respite
After the woe he had suffered. The war-worthy hero

25   Sword.

With a troop of retainers trod then the pavement
(The hall-building groaned), till he greeted the wise one,
The earl of the Ingwins; asked if the night had
Fully refreshed him, as fain he would have it.

TWENTY ONE

Hrothgar's Account of the Monsters

HROTHGAR REJOINED, helm of the Scyldings:
"Ask not of joyance! Grief is renewed to
The folk of the Danemen. Dead is Aeschere,
Yrmenlaf's brother, older than he,
My true-hearted counsellor, trusty adviser,
Shoulder-companion, when fighting in battle
Our heads we protected, when troopers were clashing,
And heroes were dashing; such an earl should be ever,
An erst-worthy[26] atheling, as Aeschere proved him.
The flickering death-spirit became in Heorot
His hand-to-hand murderer; I can not tell whither
The cruel one turned in the carcass exulting,
By cramming discovered. The quarrel she wreaked then,
That last night igone Grendel thou killedst
In gruesomest manner, with grim-holding clutches,
Since too long he had lessened my liege-troop and wasted
My folk-men so foully. He fell in the battle
With forfeit of life, and another has followed,
A mighty crime-worker, her kinsman avenging,
And henceforth hath 'stablished her hatred unyielding,
As it well may appear to many a liegeman,
Who mourneth in spirit the treasure-bestower,
Her heavy heart-sorrow; the hand is now lifeless
Which availed you in every wish that you cherished.
Land-people heard I, liegemen, this saying,

---

26   Worthy for a long time past.

Dwellers in halls, they had seen very often
A pair of such mighty march-striding creatures,
Far-dwelling spirits, holding the moorlands:
One of them wore, as well they might notice,
The image of woman, the other one wretched
In guise of a man wandered in exile,
Except he was huger than any of earthmen;
Earth-dwelling people entitled him Grendel
In days of yore: they know not their father,
Whe'r ill-going spirits any were borne him
Ever before. They guard the wolf-coverts,
Lands inaccessible, wind-beaten nesses,
Fearfullest fen-deeps, where a flood from the mountains
'Neath mists of the nesses netherward rattles,
The stream under earth: not far is it henceward
Measured by mile-lengths that the mere-water standeth,
Which forests hang over, with frost-whiting covered,
A firm-rooted forest, the floods overshadow.
There ever at night one an ill-meaning portent
A fire-flood may see; 'mong children of men
None liveth so wise that wot of the bottom;
Though harassed by hounds the heath-stepper seek for,
Fly to the forest, firm-antlered he-deer,
Spurred from afar, his spirit he yieldeth,
His life on the shore, ere in he will venture
To cover his head. Uncanny the place is:
Thence upward ascendeth the surging of waters,
Wan to the welkin, when the wind is stirring
The weathers unpleasing, till the air groweth gloomy,
And the heavens lower. Now is help to be gotten
From thee and thee only! The abode thou know'st not,
The dangerous place where thou'rt able to meet with
The sin-laden hero: seek if thou darest!
For the feud I will fully fee thee with money,
With old-time treasure, as erstwhile I did thee,
With well-twisted jewels, if away thou shalt get thee."

TWENTY TWO

Beowulf Seeks Grendel's Mother

Beowulf answered, Ecgtheow's son:
"Grieve not, O wise one! for each it is better,
His friend to avenge than with vehemence wail him;
Each of us must the end-day abide of
His earthly existence; who is able accomplish
Glory ere death! To battle-thane noble
Lifeless lying, 'tis at last most fitting.
Arise, O king, quick let us hasten
To look at the footprint of the kinsman of Grendel!
I promise thee this now: to his place he'll escape not,
To embrace of the earth, nor to mountainous forest,
Nor to depths of the ocean, wherever he wanders.
Practice thou now patient endurance
Of each of thy sorrows, as I hope for thee soothly!"
Then up sprang the old one, the All-Wielder thanked he,
Ruler Almighty, that the man had outspoken.
Then for Hrothgar a war-horse was decked with a bridle,
Curly-maned courser. The clever folk-leader
Stately proceeded: stepped then an earl-troop
Of linden-wood bearers. Her footprints were seen then
Widely in wood-paths, her way o'er the bottoms,
Where she faraway fared o'er fen-country murky,
Bore away breathless the best of retainers
Who pondered with Hrothgar the welfare of country.
The son of the athelings then went o'er the stony,
Declivitous cliffs, the close-covered passes,
Narrow passages, paths unfrequented,

Nesses abrupt, nicker-haunts many;
One of a few of wise-mooded heroes,
He onward advanced to view the surroundings,
Till he found unawares woods of the mountain
O'er hoar-stones hanging, holt-wood unjoyful;
The water stood under, welling and gory.
'Twas irksome in spirit to all of the Danemen,
Friends of the Scyldings, to many a liegeman
Sad to be suffered, a sorrow unlittle
To each of the earlmen, when to Aeschere's head they
Came on the cliff. The current was seething
With blood and with gore (the troopers gazed on it).
The horn anon sang the battle-song ready.
The troop were all seated; they saw 'long the water then
Many a serpent, mere-dragons wondrous
Trying the waters, nickers a-lying
On the cliffs of the nesses, which at noonday full often
Go on the sea-deeps their sorrowful journey,
Wild-beasts and wormkind; away then they hastened
Hot-mooded, hateful, they heard the great clamor,
The war-trumpet winding. One did the Geat-prince
Sunder from earth-joys, with arrow from bowstring,
From his sea-struggle tore him, that the trusty war-missile
Pierced to his vitals; he proved in the currents
Less doughty at swimming whom death had offcarried.
Soon in the waters the wonderful swimmer
Was straitened most sorely with sword-pointed boar-spears,
Pressed in the battle and pulled to the cliff-edge;
The liegemen then looked on the loath-fashioned stranger.
Beowulf donned then his battle-equipments,
Cared little for life; inlaid and most ample,
The hand-woven corslet which could cover his body,
Must the wave-deeps explore, that war might be powerless
To harm the great hero, and the hating one's grasp might
Not peril his safety; his head was protected
By the light-flashing helmet that should mix with the bottoms,
Trying the eddies, treasure-emblazoned,
Encircled with jewels, as in seasons long past
The weapon-smith worked it, wondrously made it,
With swine-bodies fashioned it, that thenceforward no longer
Brand might bite it, and battle-sword hurt it.

And that was not least of helpers in prowess
That Hrothgar's spokesman had lent him when straitened;
And the hilted hand-sword was Hrunting entitled,
Old and most excellent 'mong all of the treasures;
Its blade was of iron, blotted with poison,
Hardened with gore; it failed not in battle
Any hero under heaven in hand who it brandished,
Who ventured to take the terrible journeys,
The battle-field sought; not the earliest occasion
That deeds of daring 'twas destined to 'complish.
Ecglaf's kinsman minded not soothly,
Exulting in strength, what erst he had spoken
Drunken with wine, when the weapon he lent to
A sword-hero bolder; himself did not venture
'Neath the strife of the currents his life to endanger,
To fame-deeds perform; there he forfeited glory,
Repute for his strength. Not so with the other
When he clad in his corslet had equipped him for battle.

TWENTY THREE

Beowulf's Fight with Grendel's Mother

BEOWULF SPAKE, Ecgtheow's son:
"Recall now, oh, famous kinsman of Healfdene,
Prince very prudent, now to part I am ready,
Gold-friend of earlmen, what erst we agreed on,
Should I lay down my life in lending thee assistance,
When my earth-joys were over, thou wouldst evermore serve me
In stead of a father; my faithful thanemen,
My trusty retainers, protect thou and care for,
Fall I in battle: and, Hrothgar belovèd,
Send unto Higelac the high-valued jewels
Thou to me hast allotted. The lord of the Geatmen
May perceive from the gold, the Hrethling may see it
When he looks on the jewels, that a gem-giver found I
Good over-measure, enjoyed him while able.
And the ancient heirloom Unferth permit thou,
The famed one to have, the heavy-sword splendid
The hard-edgèd weapon; with Hrunting to aid me,
I shall gain me glory, or grim-death shall take me."
The atheling of Geatmen uttered these words and
Heroic did hasten, not any rejoinder
Was willing to wait for; the wave-current swallowed
The doughty-in-battle. Then a day's-length elapsed ere
He was able to see the sea at its bottom.
Early she found then who fifty of winters
The course of the currents kept in her fury,

Grisly and greedy, that the grim one's dominion
Some one of men from above was exploring.
Forth did she grab them, grappled the warrior
With horrible clutches; yet no sooner she injured
His body unscathèd: the burnie out-guarded,
That she proved but powerless to pierce through the armor,
The limb-mail locked, with loath-grabbing fingers.
The sea-wolf bare then, when bottomward came she,
The ring-prince homeward, that he after was powerless
(He had daring to do it) to deal with his weapons,
But many a mere-beast tormented him swimming,
Flood-beasts no few with fierce-biting tusks did
Break through his burnie, the brave one pursued they.
The earl then discovered he was down in some cavern
Where no water whatever anywise harmed him,
And the clutch of the current could come not anear him,
Since the roofed-hall prevented; brightness a-gleaming
Fire-light he saw, flashing resplendent.
The good one saw then the sea-bottom's monster,
The mighty mere-woman; he made a great onset
With weapon-of-battle, his hand not desisted
From striking, that war-blade struck on her head then
A battle-song greedy. The stranger perceived then
The sword would not bite, her life would not injure,
But the falchion failed the folk-prince when straitened:
Erst had it often onsets encountered,
Oft cloven the helmet, the fated one's armor:
'Twas the first time that ever the excellent jewel
Had failed of its fame. Firm-mooded after,
Not heedless of valor, but mindful of glory,
Was Higelac's kinsman; the hero-chief angry
Cast then his carved-sword covered with jewels
That it lay on the earth, hard and steel-pointed;
He hoped in his strength, his hand-grapple sturdy.
So any must act whenever he thinketh
To gain him in battle glory unending,
And is reckless of living. The lord of the War-Geats
(He shrank not from battle) seized by the shoulder
The mother of Grendel; then mighty in struggle
Swung he his enemy, since his anger was kindled,
That she fell to the floor. With furious grapple

She gave him requital early thereafter,
And stretched out to grab him; the strongest of warriors
Faint-mooded stumbled, till he fell in his traces,
Foot-going champion. Then she sat on the hall-guest
And wielded her war-knife wide-bladed, flashing,
For her son would take vengeance, her one only bairn.
His breast-armor woven bode on his shoulder;
It guarded his life, the entrance defended
'Gainst sword-point and edges. Ecgtheow's son there
Had fatally journeyed, champion of Geatmen,
In the arms of the ocean, had the armor not given,
Close-woven corslet, comfort and succor,
And had God most holy not awarded the victory,
All-knowing Lord; easily did heaven's
Ruler most righteous arrange it with justice;
Uprose he erect ready for battle.

TWENTY FOUR

Beowulf Is Double-Conqueror

THEN HE SAW MID the war-gems a weapon of victory,
An ancient giant-sword, of edges a-doughty,
Glory of warriors: of weapons 'twas choicest,
Only 'twas larger than any man else was
Able to bear to the battle-encounter,
The good and splendid work of the giants.
He grasped then the sword-hilt, knight of the Scyldings,
Bold and battle-grim, brandished his ring-sword,
Hopeless of living, hotly he smote her,
That the fiend-woman's neck firmly it grappled,
Broke through her bone-joints, the bill fully pierced her
Fate-cursèd body, she fell to the ground then:
The hand-sword was bloody, the hero exulted.
The brand was brilliant, brightly it glimmered,
Just as from heaven gemlike shineth
The torch of the firmament. He glanced 'long the building,
And turned by the wall then, Higelac's vassal
Raging and wrathful raised his battle-sword
Strong by the handle. The edge was not useless
To the hero-in-battle, but he speedily wished to
Give Grendel requital for the many assaults he
Had worked on the West-Danes not once, but often,
When he slew in slumber the subjects of Hrothgar,
Swallowed down fifteen sleeping retainers
Of the folk of the Danemen, and fully as many
Carried away, a horrible prey.
He gave him requital, grim-raging champion,

When he saw on his rest-place weary of conflict
Grendel lying, of life-joys bereavèd,
As the battle at Heorot erstwhile had scathed him;
His body far bounded, a blow when he suffered,
Death having seized him, sword-smiting heavy,
And he cut off his head then. Early this noticed
The clever carles who as comrades of Hrothgar
Gazed on the sea-deeps, that the surging wave-currents
Were mightily mingled, the mere-flood was gory:
Of the good one the gray-haired together held converse,
The hoary of head, that they hoped not to see again
The atheling ever, that exulting in victory
He'd return there to visit the distinguished folk-ruler:
Then many concluded the mere-wolf had killed him.
The ninth hour came then. From the ness-edge departed
The bold-mooded Scyldings; the gold-friend of heroes
Homeward betook him. The strangers sat down then
Soul-sick, sorrowful, the sea-waves regarding:
They wished and yet weened not their well-loved friend-lord
To see any more. The sword-blade began then,
The blood having touched it, contracting and shriveling
With battle-icicles; 'twas a wonderful marvel
That it melted entirely, likest to ice when
The Father unbindeth the bond of the frost and
Unwindeth the wave-bands, He who wieldeth dominion
Of times and of tides: a truth-firm Creator.
Nor took he of jewels more in the dwelling,
Lord of the Weders, though they lay all around him,
Than the head and the handle handsome with jewels;
The brand early melted, burnt was the weapon:
So hot was the blood, the strange-spirit poisonous
That in it did perish. He early swam off then
Who had bided in combat the carnage of haters,
Went up through the ocean; the eddies were cleansèd,
The spacious expanses, when the spirit from farland
His life put aside and this short-lived existence.
The seamen's defender came swimming to land then
Doughty of spirit, rejoiced in his sea-gift,
The bulky burden which he bore in his keeping.
The excellent vassals advanced then to meet him,
To God they were grateful, were glad in their chieftain,

That to see him safe and sound was granted them.
From the high-minded hero, then, helmet and burnie
Were speedily loosened: the ocean was putrid,
The water 'neath welkin weltered with gore.
Forth did they fare, then, their footsteps retracing,
Merry and mirthful, measured the earth-way,
The highway familiar: men very daring
Bare then the head from the sea-cliff, burdening
Each of the earlmen, excellent-valiant.
Four of them had to carry with labor
The head of Grendel to the high towering gold-hall
Upstuck on the spear, till fourteen most-valiant
And battle-brave Geatmen came there going
Straight to the palace: the prince of the people
Measured the mead-ways, their mood-brave companion.
The atheling of earlmen entered the building,
Deed-valiant man, adorned with distinction,
Doughty shield-warrior, to address King Hrothgar:
Then hung by the hair, the head of Grendel
Was borne to the building, where beer-thanes were drinking,
Loth before earlmen and eke 'fore the lady:
The warriors beheld then a wonderful sight.

TWENTY FIVE

Beowulf Brings His Trophies – Hrothgar's Gratitude

BEOWULF SPAKE, offspring of Ecgtheow:
"Lo! we blithely have brought thee, bairn of Healfdene,
Prince of the Scyldings, these presents from ocean
Which thine eye looketh on, for an emblem of glory.
I came off alive from this, narrowly 'scaping:
In war 'neath the water the work with great pains I
Performed, and the fight had been finished quite nearly,
Had God not defended me. I failed in the battle
Aught to accomplish, aided by Hrunting,
Though that weapon was worthy, but the Wielder of earth-folk
Gave me willingly to see on the wall a
Heavy old hand-sword hanging in splendor
(He guided most often the lorn and the friendless),
That I swung as a weapon. The wards of the house then
I killed in the conflict (when occasion was given me).
Then the battle-sword burned, the brand that was lifted,
As the blood-current sprang, hottest of war-sweats;
Seizing the hilt, from my foes I offbore it;
I avenged as I ought to their acts of malignity,
The murder of Danemen. I then make thee this promise,
Thou'lt be able in Heorot careless to slumber
With thy throng of heroes and the thanes of thy people
Every and each, of greater and lesser,
And thou needest not fear for them from the selfsame direction
As thou formerly fearedst, oh, folk-lord of Scyldings,

End-day for earlmen." To the age-hoary man then,
The gray-haired chieftain, the gold-fashioned sword-hilt,
Old-work of giants, was thereupon given;
Since the fall of the fiends, it fell to the keeping
Of the wielder of Danemen, the wonder-smith's labor,
And the bad-mooded being abandoned this world then,
Opponent of God, victim of murder,
And also his mother; it went to the keeping
Of the best of the world-kings, where waters encircle,
Who the scot divided in Scylding dominion.
Hrothgar discoursed, the hilt he regarded,
The ancient heirloom where an old-time contention's
Beginning was graven: the gurgling currents,
The flood slew thereafter the race of the giants,
They had proved themselves daring: that people was loth to
The Lord everlasting, through lash of the billows
The Father gave them final requital.
So in letters of rune on the clasp of the handle
Gleaming and golden, 'twas graven exactly,
Set forth and said, whom that sword had been made for,
Finest of irons, who first it was wrought for,
Wreathed at its handle and gleaming with serpents.
The wise one then said (silent they all were)
Son of old Healfdene: "He may say unrefuted
Who performs 'mid the folk-men fairness and truth
(The hoary old ruler remembers the past),
That better by birth is this bairn of the nobles!
Thy fame is extended through faraway countries,
Good friend Beowulf, o'er all of the races,
Thou holdest all firmly, hero-like strength with
Prudence of spirit. I'll prove myself grateful
As before we agreed on; thou granted for long shalt
Become a great comfort to kinsmen and comrades,
A help unto heroes. Heremod became not
Such to the Scyldings, successors of Ecgwela;
He grew not to please them, but grievous destruction,
And diresome death-woes to Danemen attracted;
He slew in anger his table-companions,
Trustworthy counsellors, till he turned off lonely
From world-joys away, wide-famous ruler:
Though high-ruling heaven in hero-strength raised him,

In might exalted him, o'er men of all nations
Made him supreme, yet a murderous spirit
Grew in his bosom: he gave then no ring-gems
To the Danes after custom; endured he unjoyful
Standing the straits from strife that was raging,
Longsome folk-sorrow. Learn then from this,
Lay hold of virtue! Though laden with winters,
I have sung thee these measures. 'Tis a marvel to tell it,
How all-ruling God from greatness of spirit
Giveth wisdom to children of men,
Manor and earlship: all things He ruleth.
He often permitteth the mood-thought of man of
The illustrious lineage to lean to possessions,
Allows him earthly delights at his manor,
A high-burg of heroes to hold in his keeping,
Maketh portions of earth-folk hear him,
And a wide-reaching kingdom so that, wisdom failing him,
He himself is unable to reckon its boundaries;
He liveth in luxury, little debars him,
Nor sickness nor age, no treachery-sorrow
Becloudeth his spirit, conflict nowhere,
No sword-hate, appeareth, but all of the world doth
Wend as he wisheth; the worse he knoweth not,
Till arrant arrogance inward pervading,
Waxeth and springeth, when the warder is sleeping,
The guard of the soul: with sorrows encompassed,
Too sound is his slumber, the slayer is near him,
Who with bow and arrow aimeth in malice.

TWENTY SIX

Hrothgar Moralizes –
Rest After Labor

"THEN BRUISED IN HIS bosom he with bitter-toothed missile
Is hurt 'neath his helmet: from harmful pollution
He is powerless to shield him by the wonderful mandates
Of the loath-cursèd spirit; what too long he hath holden
Him seemeth too small, savage he hoardeth,
Nor boastfully giveth gold-plated rings,
The fate of the future flouts and forgetteth
Since God had erst given him greatness no little,
Wielder of Glory. His end-day anear,
It afterward happens that the bodily-dwelling
Fleetingly fadeth, falls into ruins;
Another lays hold who doleth the ornaments,
The nobleman's jewels, nothing lamenting,
Heedeth no terror. Oh, Beowulf dear,
Best of the heroes, from bale-strife defend thee,
And choose thee the better, counsels eternal;
Beware of arrogance, world-famous champion!
But a little-while lasts thy life-vigor's fullness;
'Twill after hap early, that illness or sword-edge
Shall part thee from strength, or the grasp of the fire,
Or the wave of the current, or clutch of the edges,
Or flight of the war-spear, or age with its horrors,
Or thine eyes' bright flashing shall fade into darkness:
'Twill happen full early, excellent hero,
That death shall subdue thee. So the Danes a half-century

I held under heaven, helped them in struggles
'Gainst many a race in middle-earth's regions,
With ash-wood and edges, that enemies none
On earth molested me. Lo! offsetting change, now,
Came to my manor, grief after joyance,
When Grendel became my constant visitor,
Inveterate hater: I from that malice
Continually travailed with trouble no little.
Thanks be to God that I gained in my lifetime,
To the Lord everlasting, to look on the gory
Head with mine eyes, after long-lasting sorrow!
Go to the bench now, battle-adornèd
Joy in the feasting: of jewels in common
We'll meet with many when morning appeareth."
The Geatman was gladsome, ganged he immediately
To go to the bench, as the clever one bade him.
Then again as before were the famous-for-prowess,
Hall-inhabiters, handsomely banqueted,
Feasted anew. The night-veil fell then
Dark o'er the warriors. The courtiers rose then;
The gray-haired was anxious to go to his slumbers,
The hoary old Scylding. Hankered the Geatman,
The champion doughty, greatly, to rest him:
An earlman early outward did lead him,
Fagged from his faring, from far-country springing,
Who for etiquette's sake all of a liegeman's
Needs regarded, such as seamen at that time
Were bounden to feel. The big-hearted rested;
The building uptowered, spacious and gilded,
The guest within slumbered, till the sable-clad raven
Blithely foreboded the beacon of heaven.
Then the bright-shining sun o'er the bottoms came going;
The warriors hastened, the heads of the peoples
Were ready to go again to their peoples,
The high-mooded farer would faraway thenceward
Look for his vessel. The valiant one bade then,
Offspring of Ecglaf, off to bear Hrunting,
To take his weapon, his well-beloved iron;
He him thanked for the gift, saying good he accounted
The war-friend and mighty, nor chid he with words then
The blade of the brand: 'twas a brave-mooded hero.

When the warriors were ready, arrayed in their trappings,
The atheling dear to the Danemen advanced then
On to the dais, where the other was sitting,
Grim-mooded hero, greeted King Hrothgar.

TWENTY SEVEN

Sorrow at Parting

BEOWULF SPAKE, Ecgtheow's offspring:
"We men of the water wish to declare now
Fared from far-lands, we're firmly determined
To seek King Higelac. Here have we fitly
Been welcomed and feasted, as heart would desire it;
Good was the greeting. If greater affection
I am anywise able ever on earth to
Gain at thy hands, ruler of heroes,
Than yet I have done, I shall quickly be ready
For combat and conflict. O'er the course of the waters
Learn I that neighbors alarm thee with terror,
As haters did whilom, I hither will bring thee
For help unto heroes henchmen by thousands.
I know as to Higelac, the lord of the Geatmen,
Though young in years, he yet will permit me,
By words and by works, ward of the people,
Fully to furnish thee forces and bear thee
My lance to relieve thee, if liegemen shall fail thee,
And help of my hand-strength; if Hrethric be treating,
Bairn of the king, at the court of the Geatmen,
He thereat may find him friends in abundance:
Faraway countries he were better to seek for
Who trusts in himself." Hrothgar discoursed then,
Making rejoinder: "These words thou hast uttered
All-knowing God hath given thy spirit!
Ne'er heard I an earlman thus early in life

More clever in speaking: thou'rt cautious of spirit,
Mighty of muscle, in mouth-answers prudent.
I count on the hope that, happen it ever
That missile shall rob thee of Hrethel's descendant,
Edge-horrid battle, and illness or weapon
Deprive thee of prince, of people's protector,
And life thou yet holdest, the Sea-Geats will never
Find a more fitting folk-lord to choose them,
Gem-ward of heroes, than *thou* mightest prove thee,
If the kingdom of kinsmen thou carest to govern.
Thy mood-spirit likes me the longer the better,
Beowulf dear: thou hast brought it to pass that
To both these peoples peace shall be common,
To Geat-folk and Danemen, the strife be suspended,
The secret assailings they suffered in yore-days;
And also that jewels be shared while I govern
The wide-stretching kingdom, and that many shall visit
Others o'er the ocean with excellent gift-gems:
The ring-adorned bark shall bring o'er the currents
Presents and love-gifts. This people I know
Tow'rd foeman and friend firmly established,
After ancient etiquette everywise blameless."
Then the warden of earlmen gave him still farther,
Kinsman of Healfdene, a dozen of jewels,
Bade him safely seek with the presents
His well-beloved people, early returning.
Then the noble-born king kissed the distinguished,
Dear-lovèd liegeman, the Dane-prince saluted him,
And claspèd his neck; tears from him fell,
From the gray-headed man: he two things expected,
Agèd and reverend, but rather the second,
That bold in council they'd meet thereafter.
The man was so dear that he failed to suppress the
Emotions that moved him, but in mood-fetters fastened
The long-famous hero longeth in secret
Deep in his spirit for the dear-beloved man
Though not a blood-kinsman. Beowulf thenceward,
Gold-splendid warrior, walked o'er the meadows
Exulting in treasure: the sea-going vessel
Riding at anchor awaited its owner.

As they pressed on their way then, the present of Hrothgar
Was frequently referred to: a folk-king indeed that
Everyway blameless, till age did debar him
The joys of his might, which hath many oft injured.

TWENTY EIGHT

The Homeward Journey –
The Two Queens

THEN THE BAND of very valiant retainers
Came to the current; they were clad all in armor,
In link-woven burnies. The land-warder noticed
The return of the earlmen, as he erstwhile had seen them;
Nowise with insult he greeted the strangers
From the naze[27] of the cliff, but rode on to meet them;
Said the bright-armored visitors vesselward traveled
Welcome to Weders. The wide-bosomed craft then
Lay on the sand, laden with armor,
With horses and jewels, the ring-stemmèd sailer:
The mast uptowered o'er the treasure of Hrothgar.
To the boat-ward a gold-bound brand he presented,
That he was afterwards honored on the ale-bench more highly
As the heirloom's owner. Set he out on his vessel,
To drive on the deep, Dane-country left he.
Along by the mast then a sea-garment fluttered,
A rope-fastened sail. The sea-boat resounded,
The wind o'er the waters the wave-floater nowise
Kept from its journey; the sea-goer traveled,
The foamy-necked floated forth o'er the currents,
The well-fashioned vessel o'er the ways of the ocean,
Till they came within sight of the cliffs of the Geatmen,
The well-known headlands. The wave-goer hastened

---

27   Edge (nose).

Driven by breezes, stood on the shore.
Prompt at the ocean, the port-ward was ready,
Who long in the past outlooked in the distance,
At water's-edge waiting well-lovèd heroes;
He bound to the bank then the broad-bosomed vessel
Fast in its fetters, lest the force of the waters
Should be able to injure the ocean-wood winsome.
Bade he up then take the treasure of princes,
Plate-gold and fretwork; not far was it thence
To go off in search of the giver of jewels:
Hrethel's son Higelac at home there remaineth,
Himself with his comrades close to the sea-coast.
The building was splendid, the king heroic,
Great in his hall, Hygd very young was,
Fine-mooded, clever, though few were the winters
That the daughter of Haereth had dwelt in the borough;
But she nowise was cringing nor niggard of presents,
Of ornaments rare, to the race of the Geatmen.
Thrytho nursed anger, excellent folk-queen,
Hot-burning hatred: no hero whatever
'Mong household companions, her husband excepted
Dared to adventure to look at the woman
With eyes in the daytime; but he knew that death-chains
Hand-wreathed were wrought him: early thereafter,
When the hand-strife was over, edges were ready,
That fierce-raging sword-point had to force a decision,
Murder-bale show. Such no womanly custom
For a lady to practise, though lovely her person,
That a weaver-of-peace, on pretence of anger
A belovèd liegeman of life should deprive.
Soothly this hindered Heming's kinsman;
Other ale-drinking earlmen asserted
That fearful folk-sorrows fewer she wrought them,
Treacherous doings, since first she was given
Adorned with gold to the war-hero youthful,
For her origin honored, when Offa's great palace
O'er the fallow flood by her father's instructions
She sought on her journey, where she afterwards fully,
Famed for her virtue, her fate on the king's-seat
Enjoyed in her lifetime, love did she hold with
The ruler of heroes, the best, it is told me,

Of all of the earthmen that oceans encompass,
Of earl-kindreds endless; hence Offa was famous
Far and widely, by gifts and by battles,
Spear-valiant hero; the home of his fathers
He governed with wisdom, whence Eomaer did issue
For help unto heroes, Heming's kinsman,
Grandson of Garmund, great in encounters.

TWENTY NINE

Beowulf and Higelac

THEN THE BRAVE ONE DEPARTED, his band along with him,
Seeking the sea-shore, the sea-marches treading,
The wide-stretching shores. The world-candle glimmered,
The sun from the southward; they proceeded then onward,
Early arriving where they heard that the troop-lord,
Ongentheow's slayer, excellent, youthful
Folk-prince and warrior was distributing jewels,
Close in his castle. The coming of Beowulf
Was announced in a message quickly to Higelac,
That the folk-troop's defender forth to the palace
The linden-companion alive was advancing,
Secure from the combat courtward a-going.
The building was early inward made ready
For the foot-going guests as the good one had ordered.
He sat by the man then who had lived through the struggle,
Kinsman by kinsman, when the king of the people
Had in lordly language saluted the dear one,
In words that were formal. The daughter of Haereth
Coursed through the building, carrying mead-cups:
She loved the retainers, tendered the beakers
To the high-minded Geatmen. Higelac 'gan then
Pleasantly plying his companion with questions
In the high-towering palace. A curious interest
Tormented his spirit, what meaning to see in
The Sea-Geats' adventures: "Beowulf worthy,
How throve your journeying, when thou thoughtest suddenly

Far o'er the salt-streams to seek an encounter,
A battle at Heorot? Hast bettered for Hrothgar,
The famous folk-leader, his far-published sorrows
Any at all? In agony-billows
I mused upon torture, distrusted the journey
Of the belovèd liegeman; I long time did pray thee
By no means to seek out the murderous spirit,
To suffer the South-Danes themselves to decide on
Grappling with Grendel. To God I am thankful
To be suffered to see thee safe from thy journey."
Beowulf answered, bairn of old Ecgtheow:
"'Tis hidden by no means, Higelac chieftain,
From many of men, the meeting so famous,
What mournful moments of me and of Grendel
Were passed in the place where he pressing affliction
On the Victory-Scyldings scathefully brought,
Anguish forever; that all I avengèd,
So that any under heaven of the kinsmen of Grendel
Needeth not boast of that cry-in-the-morning,
Who longest liveth of the loth-going kindred,
Encompassed by moorland. I came in my journey
To the royal ring-hall, Hrothgar to greet there:
Soon did the famous scion of Healfdene,
When he understood fully the spirit that led me,
Assign me a seat with the son of his bosom.
The troop was in joyance; mead-glee greater
'Neath arch of the ether not ever beheld I
'Mid hall-building holders. The highly-famed queen,
Peace-tie of peoples, oft passed through the building,
Cheered the young troopers; she oft tendered a hero
A beautiful ring-band, ere she went to her sitting.
Oft the daughter of Hrothgar in view of the courtiers
To the earls at the end the ale-vessel carried,
Whom Freaware I heard then hall-sitters title,
When nail-adorned jewels she gave to the heroes:
Gold-bedecked, youthful, to the glad son of Froda
Her faith has been plighted; the friend of the Scyldings,
The guard of the kingdom, hath given his sanction,
And counts it a vantage, for a part of the quarrels,
A portion of hatred, to pay with the woman.

Somewhere not rarely, when the ruler has fallen,
The life-taking lance relaxeth its fury
For a brief breathing-spell, though the bride be charming!

THIRTY

Beowulf Narrates
His Adventures to Higelac

"It well may discomfit the prince of the Heathobards
And each of the thanemen of earls that attend him,
When he goes to the building escorting the woman,
That a noble-born Daneman the knights should be feasting:
There gleam on his person the leavings of elders
Hard and ring-bright, Heathobards' treasure,
While they wielded their arms, till they misled to the battle
Their own dear lives and belovèd companions.
He saith at the banquet who the collar beholdeth,
An ancient ash-warrior who earlmen's destruction
Clearly recalleth (cruel his spirit),
Sadly beginneth sounding the youthful
Thane-champion's spirit through the thoughts of his bosom,
War-grief to waken, and this word-answer speaketh:
'Art thou able, my friend, to know when thou seest it
The brand which thy father bare to the conflict
In his latest adventure, 'neath visor of helmet,
The dearly-loved iron, where Danemen did slay him,
And brave-mooded Scyldings, on the fall of the heroes,
(When vengeance was sleeping) the slaughter-place wielded?
E'en now some man of the murderer's progeny
Exulting in ornaments enters the building,
Boasts of his blood-shedding, offbeareth the jewel
Which thou shouldst wholly hold in possession!'

So he urgeth and mindeth on every occasion
With woe-bringing words, till waxeth the season
When the woman's thane for the works of his father,
The bill having bitten, blood-gory sleepeth,
Fated to perish; the other one thenceward
'Scapeth alive, the land knoweth thoroughly.
Then the oaths of the earlmen on each side are broken,
When rancors unresting are raging in Ingeld
And his wife-love waxeth less warm after sorrow.
So the Heathobards' favor not faithful I reckon,
Their part in the treaty not true to the Danemen,
Their friendship not fast. I further shall tell thee
More about Grendel, that thou fully mayst hear,
Ornament-giver, what afterward came from
The hand-rush of heroes. When heaven's bright jewel
O'er earthfields had glided, the stranger came raging,
The horrible night-fiend, us for to visit,
Where wholly unharmed the hall we were guarding.
To Hondscio happened a hopeless contention,
Death to the doomed one, dead he fell foremost,
Girded war-champion; to him Grendel became then,
To the vassal distinguished, a tooth-weaponed murderer,
The well-beloved henchman's body all swallowed.
Not the earlier off empty of hand did
The bloody-toothed murderer, mindful of evils,
Wish to escape from the gold-giver's palace,
But sturdy of strength he strove to outdo me,
Hand-ready grappled. A glove was suspended
Spacious and wondrous, in art-fetters fastened,
Which was fashioned entirely by touch of the craftman
From the dragon's skin by the devil's devices:
He down in its depths would do me unsadly
One among many, deed-doer raging,
Though sinless he saw me; not so could it happen
When I in my anger upright did stand.
'Tis too long to recount how requital I furnished
For every evil to the earlmen's destroyer;
'Twas there, my prince, that I proudly distinguished
Thy land with my labors. He left and retreated,
He lived his life a little while longer:

Yet his right-hand guarded his footstep in Heorot,
And sad-mooded thence to the sea-bottom fell he,
Mournful in mind. For the might-rush of battle
The friend of the Scyldings, with gold that was plated,
With ornaments many, much requited me,
When daylight had dawned, and down to the banquet
We had sat us together. There was chanting and joyance:
The age-stricken Scylding asked many questions
And of old-times related; oft light-ringing harp-strings,
Joy-telling wood, were touched by the brave one;
Now he uttered measures, mourning and truthful,
Then the large-hearted land-king a legend of wonder
Truthfully told us. Now troubled with years
The age-hoary warrior afterward began to
Mourn for the might that marked him in youth-days;
His breast within boiled, when burdened with winters
Much he remembered. From morning till night then
We joyed us therein as etiquette suffered,
Till the second night season came unto earth-folk.
Then early thereafter, the mother of Grendel
Was ready for vengeance, wretched she journeyed;
Her son had death ravished, the wrath of the Geatmen.
The horrible woman avengèd her offspring,
And with mighty main-strength murdered a hero.
There the spirit of Aeschere, agèd adviser,
Was ready to vanish; nor when morn had lightened
Were they anywise suffered to consume him with fire,
Folk of the Danemen, the death-weakened hero,
Nor the belovèd liegeman to lay on the pyre;
She the corpse had offcarried in the clutch of the foeman
'Neath mountain-brook's flood. To Hrothgar 'twas saddest
Of pains that ever had preyed on the chieftain;
By the life of thee the land-prince then me
Besought very sadly, in sea-currents' eddies
To display my prowess, to peril my safety,
Might-deeds accomplish; much did he promise.
I found then the famous flood-current's cruel,
Horrible depth-warder. A while unto us two
Hand was in common; the currents were seething
With gore that was clotted, and Grendel's fierce mother's

Head I offhacked in the hall at the bottom
With huge-reaching sword-edge, hardly I wrested
My life from her clutches; not doomed was I then,
But the warden of earlmen afterward gave me
Jewels in quantity, kinsman of Healfdene.

THIRTY ONE

Gift-Giving Is Mutual

"So the belovèd land-prince lived in decorum;
I had missed no rewards, no meeds of my prowess,
But he gave me jewels, regarding my wishes,
Healfdene his bairn; I'll bring them to thee, then,
Atheling of earlmen, offer them gladly.
And still unto thee is all my affection:
But few of my folk-kin find I surviving
But thee, dear Higelac!" Bade he in then to carry
The boar-image, banner, battle-high helmet,
Iron-gray armor, the excellent weapon,
In song-measures said: "This suit-for-the-battle
Hrothgar presented me, bade me expressly,
Wise-mooded atheling, thereafter to tell thee
The whole of its history, said King Heregar owned it,
Dane-prince for long: yet he wished not to give then
The mail to his son, though dearly he loved him,
Hereward the hardy. Hold all in joyance!"
I heard that there followed hard on the jewels
Two braces of stallions of striking resemblance,
Dappled and yellow; he granted him usance
Of horses and treasures. So a kinsman should bear him,
No web of treachery weave for another,
Nor by cunning craftiness cause the destruction
Of trusty companion. Most precious to Higelac,
The bold one in battle, was the bairn of his sister,
And each unto other mindful of favors.

I am told that to Hygd he proffered the necklace,
Wonder-gem rare that Wealhtheow gave him,
The troop-leader's daughter, a trio of horses
Slender and saddle-bright; soon did the jewel
Embellish her bosom, when the beer-feast was over.
So Ecgtheow's bairn brave did prove him,
War-famous man, by deeds that were valiant,
He lived in honor, belovèd companions
Slew not carousing; his mood was not cruel,
But by hand-strength hugest of heroes then living
The brave one retained the bountiful gift that
The Lord had allowed him. Long was he wretched,
So that sons of the Geatmen accounted him worthless,
And the lord of the liegemen loth was to do him
Mickle of honor, when mead-cups were passing;
They fully believed him idle and sluggish,
An indolent atheling: to the honor-blest man there
Came requital for the cuts he had suffered.
The folk-troop's defender bade fetch to the building
The heirloom of Hrethel, embellished with gold,
So the brave one enjoined it; there was jewel no richer
In the form of a weapon 'mong Geats of that era;
In Beowulf's keeping he placed it and gave him
Seven of thousands, manor and lordship.
Common to both was land 'mong the people,
Estate and inherited rights and possessions,
To the second one specially spacious dominions,
To the one who was better. It afterward happened
In days that followed, befell the battle-thanes,
After Higelac's death, and when Heardred was murdered
With weapons of warfare 'neath well-covered targets,
When valiant battle-men in victor-band sought him,
War-Scylfing heroes harassed the nephew
Of Hereric in battle. To Beowulf's keeping
Turned there in time extensive dominions:
He fittingly ruled them a fifty of winters
(He a man-ruler wise was, manor-ward old) till
A certain one 'gan, on gloom-darkening nights, a
Dragon, to govern, who guarded a treasure,
A high-rising stone-cliff, on heath that was grayish:

A path 'neath it lay, unknown unto mortals.
Some one of earthmen entered the mountain,
The heathenish hoard laid hold of with ardor;

THIRTY TWO

The Hoard and the Dragon

:

HE SOUGHT OF HIMSELF who sorely did harm him,
But, for need very pressing, the servant of one of
The sons of the heroes hate-blows evaded,
Seeking for shelter and the sin-driven warrior
Took refuge within there. He early looked in it,

:

:

⊠ when the onset surprised him,
He a gem-vessel saw there: many of suchlike
Ancient ornaments in the earth-cave were lying,
As in days of yore some one of men of
Illustrious lineage, as a legacy monstrous,
There had secreted them, careful and thoughtful,
Dear-valued jewels. Death had offsnatched them,
In the days of the past, and the one man moreover
Of the flower of the folk who fared there the longest,
Was fain to defer it, friend-mourning warder,
A little longer to be left in enjoyment
Of long-lasting treasure. A barrow all-ready
Stood on the plain the stream-currents nigh to,
New by the ness-edge, unnethe[28] of approaching:
The keeper of rings carried within a
Ponderous deal of the treasure of nobles,
Of gold that was beaten, briefly he spake then:

28   Difficult.

"Hold thou, O Earth, now heroes no more may,
The earnings of earlmen. Lo! erst in thy bosom
Worthy men won them; war-death hath ravished,
Perilous life-bale, all my warriors,
Liegemen belovèd, who this life have forsaken,
Who hall-pleasures saw. No sword-bearer have I,
And no one to burnish the gold-plated vessel,
The high-valued beaker: my heroes are vanished.
The hardy helmet behung with gilding
Shall be reaved of its riches: the ring-cleansers slumber
Who were charged to have ready visors-for-battle,
And the burnie that bided in battle-encounter
O'er breaking of war-shields the bite of the edges
Moulds with the hero. The ring-twisted armor,
Its lord being lifeless, no longer may journey
Hanging by heroes; harp-joy is vanished,
The rapture of glee-wood, no excellent falcon
Swoops through the building, no swift-footed charger
Grindeth the gravel. A grievous destruction
No few of the world-folk widely hath scattered!"
So, woeful of spirit one after all
Lamented mournfully, moaning in sadness
By day and by night, till death with its billows
Dashed on his spirit. Then the ancient dusk-scather
Found the great treasure standing all open,
He who flaming and fiery flies to the barrows,
Naked war-dragon, nightly escapeth
Encompassed with fire; men under heaven
Widely beheld him. 'Tis said that he looks for
The hoard in the earth, where old he is guarding
The heathenish treasure; he'll be nowise the better.
So three-hundred winters the waster of peoples
Held upon earth that excellent hoard-hall,
Till the forementioned earlman angered him bitterly:
The beat-plated beaker he bare to his chieftain
And fullest remission for all his remissness
Begged of his liegelord. Then the hoard was discovered,
The treasure was taken, his petition was granted
The lorn-mooded liegeman. His lord regarded
The old-work of earth-folk – 'twas the earliest occasion.
When the dragon awoke, the strife was renewed there;

He snuffed 'long the stone then, stout-hearted found he
The footprint of foeman; too far had he gone
With cunning craftiness close to the head of
The fire-spewing dragon. So undoomed he may 'scape from
Anguish and exile with ease who possesseth
The favor of Heaven. The hoard-warden eagerly
Searched o'er the ground then, would meet with the person
That caused him sorrow while in slumber reclining:
Gleaming and wild he oft went round the cavern,
All of it outward; not any of earthmen
Was seen in that desert. Yet he joyed in the battle,
Rejoiced in the conflict: oft he turned to the barrow,
Sought for the gem-cup; this he soon perceived then
That some man or other had discovered the gold,
The famous folk-treasure. Not fain did the hoard-ward
Wait until evening; then the ward of the barrow
Was angry in spirit, the loathèd one wished to
Pay for the dear-valued drink-cup with fire.
Then the day was done as the dragon would have it,
He no longer would wait on the wall, but departed
Fire-impelled, flaming. Fearful the start was
To earls in the land, as it early thereafter
To their giver-of-gold was grievously ended.

THIRTY THREE

Brave Though Aged –
Reminiscences

THE STRANGER BEGAN THEN to vomit forth fire,
To burn the great manor; the blaze then glimmered
For anguish to earlmen, not anything living
Was the hateful air-goer willing to leave there.
The war of the worm widely was noticed,
The feud of the foeman afar and anear,
How the enemy injured the earls of the Geatmen,
Harried with hatred: back he hied to the treasure,
To the well-hidden cavern ere the coming of daylight.
He had circled with fire the folk of those regions,
With brand and burning; in the barrow he trusted,
In the wall and his war-might: the weening deceived him.
Then straight was the horror to Beowulf published,
Early forsooth, that his own native homestead,
The best of buildings, was burning and melting,
Gift-seat of Geatmen. 'Twas a grief to the spirit
Of the good-mooded hero, the greatest of sorrows:
The wise one weened then that wielding his kingdom
'Gainst the ancient commandments, he had bitterly angered
The Lord everlasting: with lorn meditations
His bosom welled inward, as was nowise his custom.
The fire-spewing dragon fully had wasted
The fastness of warriors, the water-land outward,
The manor with fire. The folk-ruling hero,
Prince of the Weders, was planning to wreak him.

The warmen's defender bade them to make him,
Earlmen's atheling, an excellent war-shield
Wholly of iron: fully he knew then
That wood from the forest was helpless to aid him,
Shield against fire. The long-worthy ruler
Must live the last of his limited earth-days,
Of life in the world and the worm along with him,
Though he long had been holding hoard-wealth in plenty.
Then the ring-prince disdained to seek with a war-band,
With army extensive, the air-going ranger;
He felt no fear of the foeman's assaults and
He counted for little the might of the dragon,
His power and prowess: for previously dared he
A heap of hostility, hazarded dangers,
War-thane, when Hrothgar's palace he cleansèd,
Conquering combatant, clutched in the battle
The kinsmen of Grendel, of kindred detested.
'Twas of hand-fights not least where Higelac was slaughtered,
When the king of the Geatmen with clashings of battle,
Friend-lord of folks in Frisian dominions,
Offspring of Hrethrel perished through sword-drink,
With battle-swords beaten; thence Beowulf came then
On self-help relying, swam through the waters;
He bare on his arm, lone-going, thirty
Outfits of armor, when the ocean he mounted.
The Hetwars by no means had need to be boastful
Of their fighting afoot, who forward to meet him
Carried their war-shields: not many returned from
The brave-mooded battle-knight back to their homesteads.
Ecgtheow's bairn o'er the bight-courses swam then,
Lone-goer lorn to his land-folk returning,
Where Hygd to him tendered treasure and kingdom,
Rings and dominion: her son she not trusted,
To be able to keep the kingdom devised him
'Gainst alien races, on the death of King Higelac.
Yet the sad ones succeeded not in persuading the atheling
In any way ever, to act as a suzerain
To Heardred, or promise to govern the kingdom;
Yet with friendly counsel in the folk he sustained him,
Gracious, with honor, till he grew to be older,
Wielded the Weders. Wide-fleeing outlaws,

Ohthere's sons, sought him o'er the waters:
They had stirred a revolt 'gainst the helm of the Scylfings,
The best of the sea-kings, who in Swedish dominions
Distributed treasure, distinguished folk-leader.
'Twas the end of his earth-days; injury fatal
By swing of the sword he received as a greeting,
Offspring of Higelac; Ongentheow's bairn
Later departed to visit his homestead,
When Heardred was dead; let Beowulf rule them,
Govern the Geatmen: good was that folk-king.

THIRTY FOUR

Beowulf Seeks the Dragon – Beowulf's Reminiscences

HE PLANNED REQUITAL for the folk-leader's ruin
In days thereafter, to Eadgils the wretched
Becoming an enemy. Ohthere's son then
Went with a war-troop o'er the wide-stretching currents
With warriors and weapons: with woe-journeys cold he
After avenged him, the king's life he took.
So he came off uninjured from all of his battles,
Perilous fights, offspring of Ecgtheow,
From his deeds of daring, till that day most momentous
When he fate-driven fared to fight with the dragon.
With eleven companions the prince of the Geatmen
Went lowering with fury to look at the fire-drake:
Inquiring he'd found how the feud had arisen,
Hate to his heroes; the highly-famed gem-vessel
Was brought to his keeping through the hand of th' informer.
That in the throng was thirteenth of heroes,
That caused the beginning of conflict so bitter,
Captive and wretched, must sad-mooded thenceward
Point out the place: he passed then unwillingly
To the spot where he knew of the notable cavern,
The cave under earth, not far from the ocean,
The anger of eddies, which inward was full of
Jewels and wires: a warden uncanny,
Warrior weaponed, wardered the treasure,
Old under earth; no easy possession

For any of earth-folk access to get to.
Then the battle-brave atheling sat on the naze-edge,
While the gold-friend of Geatmen gracious saluted
His fireside-companions: woe was his spirit,
Death-boding, wav'ring; Weird very near him,
Who must seize the old hero, his soul-treasure look for,
Dragging aloof his life from his body:
Not flesh-hidden long was the folk-leader's spirit.
Beowulf spake, Ecgtheow's son:
"I survived in my youth-days many a conflict,
Hours of onset: that all I remember.
I was seven-winters old when the jewel-prince took me,
High-lord of heroes, at the hands of my father,
Hrethel the hero-king had me in keeping,
Gave me treasure and feasting, our kinship remembered;
Not ever was I *any* less dear to him
Knight in the boroughs, than the bairns of his household,
Herebald and Haethcyn and Higelac mine.
To the eldest unjustly by acts of a kinsman
Was murder-bed strewn, since him Haethcyn from horn-bow
His sheltering chieftain shot with an arrow,
Erred in his aim and injured his kinsman,
One brother the other, with blood-sprinkled spear:
'Twas a feeless fight, finished in malice,
Sad to his spirit; the folk-prince however
Had to part from existence with vengeance untaken.
So to hoar-headed hero 'tis heavily crushing
To live to see his son as he rideth
Young on the gallows: then measures he chanteth,
A song of sorrow, when his son is hanging
For the raven's delight, and aged and hoary
He is unable to offer any assistance.
Every morning his offspring's departure
Is constant recalled: he cares not to wait for
The birth of an heir in his borough-enclosures,
Since that one through death-pain the deeds hath experienced.
He heart-grieved beholds in the house of his son the
Wine-building wasted, the wind-lodging places
Reaved of their roaring; the riders are sleeping,
The knights in the grave; there's no sound of the harp-wood,
Joy in the yards, as of yore were familiar.

THIRTY FIVE

Reminiscences (Continued) – Beowulf's Last Battle

"HE SEEKS THEN HIS chamber, singeth a woe-song
One for the other; all too extensive
Seemed homesteads and plains. So the helm of the Weders
Mindful of Herebald heart-sorrow carried,
Stirred with emotion, nowise was able
To wreak his ruin on the ruthless destroyer:
He was unable to follow the warrior with hatred,
With deeds that were direful, though dear he not held him.
Then pressed by the pang this pain occasioned him,
He gave up glee, God-light elected;
He left to his sons, as the man that is rich does,
His land and fortress, when from life he departed.
Then was crime and hostility 'twixt Swedes and Geatmen,
O'er wide-stretching water warring was mutual,
Burdensome hatred, when Hrethel had perished,
And Ongentheow's offspring were active and valiant,
Wished not to hold to peace oversea, but
Round Hreosna-beorh often accomplished
Cruelest massacre. This my kinsman avengèd,
The feud and fury, as 'tis found on inquiry,
Though one of them paid it with forfeit of life-joys,
With price that was hard: the struggle became then
Fatal to Haethcyn, lord of the Geatmen.
Then I heard that at morning one brother the other
With edges of irons egged on to murder,

Where Ongentheow maketh onset on Eofor:
The helmet crashed, the hoary-haired Scylfing
Sword-smitten fell, his hand then remembered
Feud-hate sufficient, refused not the death-blow.
The gems that he gave me, with jewel-bright sword I
'Quited in contest, as occasion was offered:
Land he allowed me, life-joy at homestead,
Manor to live on. Little he needed
From Gepids or Danes or in Sweden to look for
Trooper less true, with treasure to buy him;
'Mong foot-soldiers ever in front I would hie me,
Alone in the vanguard, and evermore gladly
Warfare shall wage, while this weapon endureth
That late and early often did serve me
When I proved before heroes the slayer of Daeghrefn,
Knight of the Hugmen: he by no means was suffered
To the king of the Frisians to carry the jewels,
The breast-decoration; but the banner-possessor
Bowed in the battle, brave-mooded atheling.
No weapon was slayer, but war-grapple broke then
The surge of his spirit, his body destroying.
Now shall weapon's edge make war for the treasure,
And hand and firm-sword." Beowulf spake then,
Boast-words uttered – the latest occasion:
"I braved in my youth-days battles unnumbered;
Still am I willing the struggle to look for,
Fame-deeds perform, folk-warden prudent,
If the hateful despoiler forth from his cavern
Seeketh me out!" Each of the heroes,
Helm-bearers sturdy, he thereupon greeted
Belovèd co-liegemen – his last salutation:
"No brand would I bear, no blade for the dragon,
Wist I a way my word-boast to 'complish
Else with the monster, as with Grendel I did it;
But fire in the battle hot I expect there,
Furious flame-burning: so I fixed on my body
Target and war-mail. The ward of the barrow
I'll not flee from a foot-length, the foeman uncanny.
At the wall 'twill befall us as Fate decreeth,
Each one's Creator. I am eager in spirit,
With the wingèd war-hero to away with all boasting.

Bide on the barrow with burnies protected,
Earls in armor, which of *us* two may better
Bear his disaster, when the battle is over.
'Tis no matter of yours, and man cannot do it,
But me and me only, to measure his strength with
The monster of malice, might-deeds to 'complish.
I with prowess shall gain the gold, or the battle,
Direful death-woe will drag off your ruler!"
The mighty champion rose by his shield then,
Brave under helmet, in battle-mail went he
'Neath steep-rising stone-cliffs, the strength he relied on
Of one man alone: no work for a coward.
Then he saw by the wall who a great many battles
Had lived through, most worthy, when foot-troops collided,
Stone-arches standing, stout-hearted champion,
Saw a brook from the barrow bubbling out thenceward:
The flood of the fountain was fuming with war-flame:
Not nigh to the hoard, for season the briefest
Could he brave, without burning, the abyss that was yawning,
The drake was so fiery. The prince of the Weders
Caused then that words came from his bosom,
So fierce was his fury; the firm-hearted shouted:
His battle-clear voice came in resounding
'Neath the gray-colored stone. Stirred was his hatred,
The hoard-ward distinguished the speech of a man;
Time was no longer to look out for friendship.
The breath of the monster issued forth first,
Vapory war-sweat, out of the stone-cave:
The earth re-echoed. The earl 'neath the barrow
Lifted his shield, lord of the Geatmen,
Tow'rd the terrible stranger: the ring-twisted creature's
Heart was then ready to seek for a struggle.
The excellent battle-king first brandished his weapon,
The ancient heirloom, of edges unblunted,
To the death-planners twain was terror from other.
The lord of the troopers intrepidly stood then
'Gainst his high-rising shield, when the dragon coiled him
Quickly together: in corslet he bided.
He went then in blazes, bended and striding,
Hasting him forward. His life and body
The targe well protected, for time-period shorter

Than wish demanded for the well-renowned leader,
Where he then for the first day was forced to be victor,
Famous in battle, as Fate had not willed it.
The lord of the Geatmen uplifted his hand then,
Smiting the fire-drake with sword that was precious,
That bright on the bone the blade-edge did weaken,
Bit more feebly than his folk-leader needed,
Burdened with bale-griefs. Then the barrow-protector,
When the sword-blow had fallen, was fierce in his spirit,
Flinging his fires, flamings of battle
Gleamed then afar: the gold-friend of Weders
Boasted no conquests, his battle-sword failed him
Naked in conflict, as by no means it ought to,
Long-trusty weapon. 'Twas no slight undertaking
That Ecgtheow's famous offspring would leave
The drake-cavern's bottom; he must live in some region
Other than this, by the will of the dragon,
As each one of earthmen existence must forfeit.
'Twas early thereafter the excellent warriors
Met with each other. Anew and afresh
The hoard-ward took heart (gasps heaved then his bosom):
Sorrow he suffered encircled with fire
Who the people erst governed. His companions by no means
Were banded about him, bairns of the princes,
With valorous spirit, but they sped to the forest,
Seeking for safety. The soul-deeps of one were
Ruffled by care: kin-love can never
Aught in him waver who well doth consider.

THIRTY SIX

Wiglaf the Trusty – Beowulf is Deserted by Friends and by Sword

THE SON OF WEOHSTAN was Wiglaf entitled,
Shield-warrior precious, prince of the Scylfings,
Aelfhere's kinsman: he saw his dear liegelord
Enduring the heat 'neath helmet and visor.
Then he minded the holding that erst he had given him,
The Waegmunding warriors' wealth-blessèd homestead,
Each of the folk-rights his father had wielded;
He was hot for the battle, his hand seized the target,
The yellow-bark shield, he unsheathed his old weapon,
Which was known among earthmen as the relic of Eanmund,
Ohthere's offspring, whom, exiled and friendless,
Weohstan did slay with sword-edge in battle,
And carried his kinsman the clear-shining helmet,
The ring-made burnie, the old giant-weapon
That Onela gave him, his boon-fellow's armor,
Ready war-trappings: he the feud did not mention,
Though he'd fatally smitten the son of his brother.
Many a half-year held he the treasures,
The bill and the burnie, till his bairn became able,
Like his father before him, fame-deeds to 'complish;
Then he gave him 'mong Geatmen a goodly array of
Weeds for his warfare; he went from life then
Old on his journey. 'Twas the earliest time then
That the youthful champion might charge in the battle
Aiding his liegelord; his spirit was dauntless.

Nor did kinsman's bequest quail at the battle:
This the dragon discovered on their coming together.
Wiglaf uttered many a right-saying,
Said to his fellows, sad was his spirit:
"I remember the time when, tasting the mead-cup,
We promised in the hall the lord of us all
Who gave us these ring-treasures, that this battle-equipment,
Swords and helmets, we'd certainly quite him,
Should need of such aid ever befall him:
In the war-band he chose us for this journey spontaneously,
Stirred us to glory and gave me these jewels,
Since he held and esteemed us trust-worthy spearmen,
Hardy helm-bearers, though this hero-achievement
Our lord intended alone to accomplish,
Ward of his people, for most of achievements,
Doings audacious, he did among earth-folk.
The day is now come when the ruler of earthmen
Needeth the vigor of valiant heroes:
Let us wend us towards him, the war-prince to succor,
While the heat yet rageth, horrible fire-fight.
God wot in me, 'tis mickle the liefer
The blaze should embrace my body and eat it
With my treasure-bestower. Meseemeth not proper
To bear our battle-shields back to our country,
'Less first we are able to fell and destroy the
Long-hating foeman, to defend the life of
The prince of the Weders. Well do I know 'tisn't
Earned by his exploits, he only of Geatmen
Sorrow should suffer, sink in the battle:
Brand and helmet to us both shall be common,
Shield-cover, burnie." Through the bale-smoke he stalked then,
Went under helmet to the help of his chieftain,
Briefly discoursing: "Beowulf dear,
Perform thou all fully, as thou formerly saidst,
In thy youthful years, that while yet thou livedst
Thou wouldst let thine honor not ever be lessened.
Thy life thou shalt save, mighty in actions,
Atheling undaunted, with all of thy vigor;
I'll give thee assistance." The dragon came raging,
Wild-mooded stranger, when these words had been uttered
('Twas the second occasion), seeking his enemies,

Men that were hated, with hot-gleaming fire-waves;
With blaze-billows burned the board to its edges:
The fight-armor failed then to furnish assistance
To the youthful spear-hero: but the young-agèd stripling
Quickly advanced 'neath his kinsman's war-target,
Since his own had been ground in the grip of the fire.
Then the warrior-king was careful of glory,
He soundly smote with sword-for-the-battle,
That it stood in the head by hatred driven;
Naegling was shivered, the old and iron-made
Brand of Beowulf in battle deceived him.
'Twas denied him that edges of irons were able
To help in the battle; the hand was too mighty
Which every weapon, as I heard on inquiry,
Outstruck in its stroke, when to struggle he carried
The wonderful war-sword: it waxed him no better.
Then the people-despoiler – third of his onsets –
Fierce-raging fire-drake, of feud-hate was mindful,
Charged on the strong one, when chance was afforded,
Heated and war-grim, seized on his neck
With teeth that were bitter; he bloody did wax with
Soul-gore seething; sword-blood in waves boiled.

THIRTY SEVEN

The Fatal Struggle – Beowulf's Last Moments

THEN I HEARD THAT at need of the king of the people
The upstanding earlman exhibited prowess,
Vigor and courage, as suited his nature;
He his head did not guard, but the high-minded liegeman's
Hand was consumed, when he succored his kinsman,
So he struck the strife-bringing strange-comer lower,
Earl-thane in armor, that *in* went the weapon
Gleaming and plated, that 'gan then the fire
Later to lessen. The liegelord himself then
Retained his consciousness, brandished his war-knife,
Battle-sharp, bitter, that he bare on his armor:
The Weder-lord cut the worm in the middle.
They had felled the enemy (life drove out then
Puissant prowess), the pair had destroyed him,
Land-chiefs related: so a liegeman should prove him,
A thaneman when needed. To the prince 'twas the last of
His era of conquest by his own great achievements,
The latest of world-deeds. The wound then began
Which the earth-dwelling dragon erstwhile had wrought him
To burn and to swell. He soon then discovered
That bitterest bale-woe in his bosom was raging,
Poison within. The atheling advanced then,
That along by the wall, he prudent of spirit
Might sit on a settle; he saw the giant-work,
How arches of stone strengthened with pillars

The earth-hall eternal inward supported.
Then the long-worthy liegeman laved with his hand the
Far-famous chieftain, gory from sword-edge,
Refreshing the face of his friend-lord and ruler,
Sated with battle, unbinding his helmet.
Beowulf answered, of his injury spake he,
His wound that was fatal (he was fully aware
He had lived his allotted life-days enjoying
The pleasures of earth; then past was entirely
His measure of days, death very near):
"My son I would give now my battle-equipments,
Had any of heirs been after me granted,
Along of my body. This people I governed
Fifty of winters: no king 'mong my neighbors
Dared to encounter me with comrades-in-battle,
Try me with terror. The time to me ordered
I bided at home, mine own kept fitly,
Sought me no snares, swore me not many
Oaths in injustice. Joy over all this
I'm able to have, though ill with my death-wounds;
Hence the Ruler of Earthmen need not charge me
With the killing of kinsmen, when cometh my life out
Forth from my body. Fare thou with haste now
To behold the hoard 'neath the hoar-grayish stone,
Well-lovèd Wiglaf, now the worm is a-lying,
Sore-wounded sleepeth, disseized of his treasure.
Go thou in haste that treasures of old I,
Gold-wealth may gaze on, together see lying
The ether-bright jewels, be easier able,
Having the heap of hoard-gems, to yield my
Life and the land-folk whom long I have governed."

THIRTY EIGHT

Wiglaf Plunders the Dragon's Den – Beowulf's Death

THEN HEARD I THAT Wihstan's son very quickly,
These words being uttered, heeded his liegelord
Wounded and war-sick, went in his armor,
His well-woven ring-mail, 'neath the roof of the barrow.
Then the trusty retainer treasure-gems many
Victorious saw, when the seat he came near to,
Gold-treasure sparkling spread on the bottom,
Wonder on the wall, and the worm-creature's cavern,
The ancient dawn-flier's, vessels a-standing,
Cups of the ancients of cleansers bereavèd,
Robbed of their ornaments: there were helmets in numbers,
Old and rust-eaten, arm-bracelets many,
Artfully woven. Wealth can easily,
Gold on the sea-bottom, turn into vanity
Each one of earthmen, arm him who pleaseth!
And he saw there lying an all-golden banner
High o'er the hoard, of hand-wonders greatest,
Linkèd with lacets: a light from it sparkled,
That the floor of the cavern he was able to look on,
To examine the jewels. Sight of the dragon
Not any was offered, but edge offcarried him.
Then I heard that the hero the hoard-treasure plundered,
The giant-work ancient reaved in the cavern,
Bare on his bosom the beakers and platters,

As himself would fain have it, and took off the standard,
The brightest of beacons; the bill had erst injured
(Its edge was of iron), the old-ruler's weapon,
Him who long had watched as ward of the jewels,
Who fire-terror carried hot for the treasure,
Rolling in battle, in middlemost darkness,
Till murdered he perished. The messenger hastened,
Not loth to return, hurried by jewels:
Curiosity urged him if, excellent-mooded,
Alive he should find the lord of the Weders
Mortally wounded, at the place where he left him.
'Mid the jewels he found then the famous old chieftain,
His liegelord belovèd, at his life's-end gory:
He thereupon 'gan to lave him with water,
Till the point of his word piercèd his breast-hoard.
Beowulf spake (the gold-gems he noticed),
The old one in sorrow: "For the jewels I look on
Thanks do I utter for all to the Ruler,
Wielder of Worship, with words of devotion,
The Lord everlasting, that He let me such treasures
Gain for my people ere death overtook me.
Since I've bartered the agèd life to me granted
For treasure of jewels, attend ye henceforward
The wants of the war-thanes; I can wait here no longer.
The battle-famed bid ye to build them a grave-hill,
Bright when I'm burned, at the brim-current's limit;
As a memory-mark to the men I have governed,
Aloft it shall tower on Whale's-Ness uprising,
That earls of the ocean hereafter may call it
Beowulf's barrow, those who barks ever-dashing
From a distance shall drive o'er the darkness of waters."
The bold-mooded troop-lord took from his neck then
The ring that was golden, gave to his liegeman,
The youthful war-hero, his gold-flashing helmet,
His collar and war-mail, bade him well to enjoy them:
"Thou art latest left of the line of our kindred,
Of Waegmunding people: Weird hath offcarried
All of my kinsmen to the Creator's glory,
Earls in their vigor: I shall after them fare."
'Twas the aged liegelord's last-spoken word in

His musings of spirit, ere he mounted the fire,
The battle-waves burning: from his bosom departed
His soul to seek the sainted ones' glory.

THIRTY NINE

The Dead Foes –
Wiglaf's Bitter Taunts

It had woefully chanced then the youthful retainer
To behold on earth the most ardent-belovèd
At his life-days' limit, lying there helpless.
The slayer too lay there, of life all bereavèd,
Horrible earth-drake, harassed with sorrow:
The round-twisted monster was permitted no longer
To govern the ring-hoards, but edges of war-swords
Mightily seized him, battle-sharp, sturdy
Leavings of hammers, that still from his wounds
The flier-from-farland fell to the earth
Hard by his hoard-house, hopped he at midnight
Not e'er through the air, nor exulting in jewels
Suffered them to see him: but he sank then to earthward
Through the hero-chief's handwork. I heard sure it throve then
But few in the land of liegemen of valor,
Though of every achievement bold he had proved him,
To run 'gainst the breath of the venomous scather,
Or the hall of the treasure to trouble with hand-blows,
If he watching had found the ward of the hoard-hall
On the barrow abiding. Beowulf's part of
The treasure of jewels was paid for with death;
Each of the twain had attained to the end of
Life so unlasting. Not long was the time till
The tardy-at-battle returned from the thicket,

The timid truce-breakers ten all together,
Who durst not before play with the lances
In the prince of the people's pressing emergency;
But blushing with shame, with shields they betook them,
With arms and armor where the old one was lying:
They gazed upon Wiglaf. He was sitting exhausted,
Foot-going fighter, not far from the shoulders
Of the lord of the people, would rouse him with water;
No whit did it help him; though he hoped for it keenly,
He was able on earth not at all in the leader
Life to retain, and nowise to alter
The will of the Wielder; the World-Ruler's power
Would govern the actions of each one of heroes,
As yet He is doing. From the young one forthwith then
Could grim-worded greeting be got for him quickly
Whose courage had failed him. Wiglaf discoursed then,
Weohstan his son, sad-mooded hero,
Looked on the hated: "He who soothness will utter
Can say that the liegelord who gave you the jewels,
The ornament-armor wherein ye are standing,
When on ale-bench often he offered to hall-men
Helmet and burnie, the prince to his liegemen,
As best upon earth he was able to find him –
That he wildly wasted his war-gear undoubtedly
When battle o'ertook him. The troop-king no need had
To glory in comrades; yet God permitted him,
Victory-Wielder, with weapon unaided
Himself to avenge, when vigor was needed.
I life-protection but little was able
To give him in battle, and I 'gan, notwithstanding,
Helping my kinsman (my strength overtaxing):
He waxed the weaker when with weapon I smote on
My mortal opponent, the fire less strongly
Flamed from his bosom. Too few of protectors
Came round the king at the critical moment.
Now must ornament-taking and weapon-bestowing,
Home-joyance all, cease for your kindred,
Food for the people; each of your warriors
Must needs be bereavèd of rights that he holdeth
In landed possessions, when faraway nobles

Shall learn of your leaving your lord so basely,
The dastardly deed. Death is more pleasant
To every earlman than infamous life is!"

FORTY

The Messenger of Death

THEN HE CHARGED THAT the battle be announced at the hedge
Up o'er the cliff-edge, where the earl-troopers bided
The whole of the morning, mood-wretched sat them,
Bearers of battle-shields, both things expecting,
The end of his lifetime and the coming again of
The liegelord belovèd. Little reserved he
Of news that was known, who the ness-cliff did travel,
But he truly discoursed to all that could hear him:
"Now the free-giving friend-lord of the folk of the Weders,
The folk-prince of Geatmen, is fast in his death-bed,
By the deeds of the dragon in death-bed abideth;
Along with him lieth his life-taking foeman
Slain with knife-wounds: he was wholly unable
To injure at all the ill-planning monster
With bite of his sword-edge. Wiglaf is sitting,
Offspring of Wihstan, up over Beowulf,
Earl o'er another whose end-day hath reached him,
Head-watch holdeth o'er heroes unliving,
For friend and for foeman. The folk now expecteth
A season of strife when the death of the folk-king
To Frankmen and Frisians in far-lands is published.
The war-hatred waxed warm 'gainst the Hugmen,
When Higelac came with an army of vessels
Faring to Friesland, where the Frankmen in battle
Humbled him and bravely with overmight 'complished
That the mail-clad warrior must sink in the battle,
Fell 'mid his folk-troop: no fret-gems presented

The atheling to earlmen; aye was denied us
Merewing's mercy. The men of the Swedelands
For truce or for truth trust I but little;
But widely 'twas known that near Ravenswood Ongentheow
Sundered Haethcyn the Hrethling from life-joys,
When for pride overweening the War-Scylfings first did
Seek the Geatmen with savage intentions.
Early did Ohthere's age-laden father,
Old and terrible, give blow in requital,
Killing the sea-king, the queen-mother rescued,
The old one his consort deprived of her gold,
Onela's mother and Ohthere's also,
And then followed the feud-nursing foemen till hardly,
Reaved of their ruler, they Ravenswood entered.
Then with vast-numbered forces he assaulted the remnant,
Weary with wounds, woe often promised
The livelong night to the sad-hearted war-troop:
Said he at morning would kill them with edges of weapons,
Some on the gallows for glee to the fowls.
Aid came after to the anxious-in-spirit
At dawn of the day, after Higelac's bugle
And trumpet-sound heard they, when the good one proceeded
And faring followed the flower of the troopers.

FORTY ONE

The Messenger's Retrospect

"THE BLOOD-STAINÈD TRACE of Swedes and Geatmen,
The death-rush of warmen, widely was noticed,
How the folks with each other feud did awaken.
The worthy one went then with well-beloved comrades,
Old and dejected to go to the fastness,
Ongentheo earl upward then turned him;
Of Higelac's battle he'd heard on inquiry,
The exultant one's prowess, despaired of resistance,
With earls of the ocean to be able to struggle,
'Gainst sea-going sailors to save the hoard-treasure,
His wife and his children; he fled after thenceward
Old 'neath the earth-wall. Then was offered pursuance
To the braves of the Swedemen, the banner to Higelac.
They fared then forth o'er the field-of-protection,
When the Hrethling heroes hedgeward had thronged them.
Then with edges of irons was Ongentheow driven,
The gray-haired to tarry, that the troop-ruler had to
Suffer the power solely of Eofor:
Wulf then wildly with weapon assaulted him,
Wonred his son, that for swinge[29] of the edges
The blood from his body burst out in currents,
Forth 'neath his hair. He feared not however,
Gray-headed Scylfing, but speedily quited
The wasting wound-stroke with worse exchange,
When the king of the thane-troop thither did turn him:

29   Stroke, blow.

The wise-mooded son of Wonred was powerless
To give a return-blow to the age-hoary man,
But his head-shielding helmet first hewed he to pieces,
That flecked with gore perforce he did totter,
Fell to the earth; not fey was he yet then,
But up did he spring though an edge-wound had reached him.
Then Higelac's vassal, valiant and dauntless,
When his brother lay dead, made his broad-bladed weapon,
Giant-sword ancient, defence of the giants,
Bound o'er the shield-wall; the folk-prince succumbed then,
Shepherd of people, was pierced to the vitals.
There were many attendants who bound up his kinsman,
Carried him quickly when occasion was granted
That the place of the slain they were suffered to manage.
This pending, one hero plundered the other,
His armor of iron from Ongentheow ravished,
His hard-sword hilted and helmet together;
The old one's equipments he carried to Higelac.
He the jewels received, and rewards 'mid the troopers
Graciously promised, and so did accomplish:
The king of the Weders requited the war-rush,
Hrethel's descendant, when home he repaired him,
To Eofor and Wulf with wide-lavished treasures,
To each of them granted a hundred of thousands
In land and rings wrought out of wire:
None upon mid-earth needed to twit him
With the gifts he gave them, when glory they conquered;
And to Eofor then gave he his one only daughter,
The honor of home, as an earnest of favor.
That's the feud and hatred – as ween I 'twill happen –
The anger of earthmen, that earls of the Swedemen
Will visit on us, when they hear that our leader
Lifeless is lying, he who longtime protected
His hoard and kingdom 'gainst hating assailers,
Who on the fall of the heroes defended of yore
The deed-mighty Scyldings, did for the troopers
What best did avail them, and further moreover
Hero-deeds 'complished. Now is haste most fitting,
That the lord of liegemen we look upon yonder,
And *that* one carry on journey to death-pyre
Who ring-presents gave us. Not aught of it all

Shall melt with the brave one – there's a mass of bright jewels,
Gold beyond measure, gruesomely purchased
And ending it all ornament-rings too
Bought with his life; these fire shall devour,
Flame shall cover, no earlman shall wear
A jewel-memento, nor beautiful virgin
Have on her neck rings to adorn her,
But wretched in spirit bereavèd of gold-gems
She shall oft with others be exiled and banished,
Since the leader of liegemen hath laughter forsaken,
Mirth and merriment. Hence many a war-spear
Cold from the morning shall be clutched in the fingers,
Heaved in the hand, no harp-music's sound shall
Waken the warriors, but the wan-coated raven
Fain over fey ones freely shall gabble,
Shall say to the eagle how he sped in the eating,
When, the wolf his companion, he plundered the slain."
So the high-minded hero was rehearsing these stories
Loathsome to hear; he lied as to few of
Weirds and of words. All the war-troop arose then,
'Neath the Eagle's Cape sadly betook them,
Weeping and woeful, the wonder to look at.
They saw on the sand then soulless a-lying,
His slaughter-bed holding, him who rings had given them
In days that were done; then the death-bringing moment
Was come to the good one, that the king very warlike,
Wielder of Weders, with wonder-death perished.
First they beheld there a creature more wondrous,
The worm on the field, in front of them lying,
The foeman before them: the fire-spewing dragon,
Ghostly and grisly guest in his terrors,
Was scorched in the fire; as he lay there he measured
Fifty of feet; came forth in the night-time
To rejoice in the air, thereafter departing
To visit his den; he in death was then fastened,
He would joy in no other earth-hollowed caverns.
There stood round about him beakers and vessels,
Dishes were lying and dear-valued weapons,
With iron-rust eaten, as in earth's mighty bosom
A thousand of winters there they had rested:
That mighty bequest then with magic was guarded,

Gold of the ancients, that earlman not any
The ring-hall could touch, save Ruling-God only,
Sooth-king of Vict'ries gave whom He wished to
(He is earth-folk's protector) to open the treasure,
E'en to such among mortals as seemed to Him proper.

FORTY TWO

Wiglaf's Sad Story –
The Hoard Carried Off

THEN 'TWAS SEEN THAT the journey prospered him little
Who wrongly within had the ornaments hidden
Down 'neath the wall. The warden erst slaughtered
Some few of the folk-troop: the feud then thereafter
Was hotly avengèd. 'Tis a wonder where,
When the strength-famous trooper has attained to the end of
Life-days allotted, then no longer the man may
Remain with his kinsmen where mead-cups are flowing.
So to Beowulf happened when the ward of the barrow,
Assaults, he sought for: himself had no knowledge
How his leaving this life was likely to happen.
So to doomsday, famous folk-leaders down did
Call it with curses – who 'complished it there –
That that man should be ever of ill-deeds convicted,
Confined in foul-places, fastened in hell-bonds,
Punished with plagues, who this place should e'er ravage.
He cared not for gold: rather the Wielder's
Favor preferred he first to get sight of.
Wiglaf discoursed then, Wihstan his son:
"Oft many an earlman on one man's account must
Sorrow endure, as to us it hath happened.
The liegelord belovèd we could little prevail on,
Kingdom's keeper, counsel to follow,
Not to go to the guardian of the gold-hoard, but let him
Lie where he long was, live in his dwelling

Till the end of the world. Met we a destiny
Hard to endure: the hoard has been looked at,
Been gained very grimly; too grievous the fate that
The prince of the people pricked to come thither.
I was therein and all of it looked at,
The building's equipments, since access was given me,
Not kindly at all entrance permitted
Within under earth-wall. Hastily seized I
And held in my hands a huge-weighing burden
Of hoard-treasures costly, hither out bare them
To my liegelord belovèd: life was yet in him,
And consciousness also; the old one discoursed then
Much and mournfully, commanded to greet you,
Bade that remembering the deeds of your friend-lord
Ye build on the fire-hill of corpses a lofty
Burial-barrow, broad and far-famous,
As 'mid world-dwelling warriors he was widely most honored
While he reveled in riches. Let us rouse us and hasten
Again to see and seek for the treasure,
The wonder 'neath wall. The way I will show you,
That close ye may look at ring-gems sufficient
And gold in abundance. Let the bier with promptness
Fully be fashioned, when forth we shall come,
And lift we our lord, then, where long he shall tarry,
Well-beloved warrior, 'neath the Wielder's protection."
Then the son of Wihstan bade orders be given,
Mood-valiant man, to many of heroes,
Holders of homesteads, that they hither from far,
Leaders of liegemen, should look for the good one
With wood for his pyre: "The flame shall now swallow
(The wan fire shall wax) the warriors' leader
Who the rain of the iron often abided,
When, sturdily hurled, the storm of the arrows
Leapt o'er linden-wall, the lance rendered service,
Furnished with feathers followed the arrow."
Now the wise-mooded son of Wihstan did summon
The best of the braves from the band of the ruler
Seven together; 'neath the enemy's roof he
Went with the seven; one of the heroes
Who fared at the front, a fire-blazing torch-light
Bare in his hand. No lot then decided

Who that hoard should havoc, when hero-earls saw it
Lying in the cavern uncared-for entirely,
Rusting to ruin: they rued then but little
That they hastily hence hauled out the treasure,
The dear-valued jewels; the dragon eke pushed they,
The worm o'er the wall, let the wave-currents take him,
The waters enwind the ward of the treasures.
There wounden gold on a wain was uploaded,
A mass unmeasured, the men-leader off then,
The hero hoary, to Whale's-Ness was carried.

FORTY THREE

The Burning of Beowulf

THE FOLK OF THE Geatmen got him then ready
A pile on the earth strong for the burning,
Behung with helmets, hero-knights' targets,
And bright-shining burnies, as he begged they should have them;
Then wailing war-heroes their world-famous chieftain,
Their liegelord beloved, laid in the middle.
Soldiers began then to make on the barrow
The largest of dead-fires: dark o'er the vapor
The smoke-cloud ascended, the sad-roaring fire,
Mingled with weeping (the wind-roar subsided)
Till the building of bone it had broken to pieces,
Hot in the heart. Heavy in spirit
They mood-sad lamented the men-leader's ruin;
And mournful measures the much-grieving widow
:
:
:
:
:
:
The men of the Weders made accordingly
A hill on the height, high and extensive,
Of sea-going sailors to be seen from a distance,
And the brave one's beacon built where the fire was,
In ten-days' space, with a wall surrounded it,
As wisest of world-folk could most worthily plan it.
They placed in the barrow rings and jewels,

All such ornaments as erst in the treasure
War-mooded men had won in possession:
The earnings of earlmen to earth they entrusted,
The gold to the dust, where yet it remaineth
As useless to mortals as in foregoing eras.
'Round the dead-mound rode then the doughty-in-battle,
Bairns of all twelve 'of the chiefs of the people,
More would they mourn, lament for their ruler,
Speak in measure, mention him with pleasure,
Weighed his worth, and his warlike achievements
Mightily commended, as 'tis meet one praise his
Liegelord in words and love him in spirit,
When forth from his body he fares to destruction.
So lamented mourning the men of the Geats,
Fond-loving vassals, the fall of their lord,
Said he was kindest of kings under heaven,
Gentlest of men, most winning of manner,
Friendliest to folk-troops and fondest of honor.

ROYAL
CLASSICS

READ THE TOP 40 ROYAL CLASSICS

20,000 Leagues Under the Sea BY JULES VERNE
A Christmas Carol BY CHARLES DICKENS
A Tale of Two Cities BY CHARLES DICKENS
Aesop's Fables BY AESOP
Alice in Wonderland BY LEWIS CARROLL
Anna Karenina BY LEO TOLSTOY
Candide BY VOLTAIRE
Crime and Punishment BY FYODOR DOSTOEVSKY
Don Quixote BY MIGUEL DE CERVANTES
Dracula BY BRAM STOKER
Frankenstein BY MARY SHELLEY
Great Expectations BY CHARLES DICKENS
Jane Eyre BY CHARLOTTE BRONTË
Les Misérables BY VICTOR HUGO
Meditations BY MARCUS AURELIUS
Moby Dick BY HERMAN MELVILLE
Paradise Lost BY JOHN MILTON
Plato: Five Dialogues BY PLATO
Pride & Prejudice BY JANE AUSTEN
The Adventures of Sherlock Holmes BY A. CONAN DOYLE
The Adventures of Tom Sawyer BY MARK TWAIN
The Art of War BY SUN TZU
The Count of Monte Cristo BY ALEXANDRE DUMAS
The Federalist Papers BY ALEXANDER HAMILTON
The Importance of Being Earnest BY OSCAR WILDE
The Odyssey BY HOMER
The Origin of Species BY CHARLES DARWIN
The Prince BY NICCOLÒ MACHIAVELLI
The Prophet BY KAHLIL GIBRAN
The Republic BY PLATO
The Three Musketeers BY ALEXANDRE DUMAS
The Time Machine BY H. G. WELLS
The Wealth of Nations BY ADAM SMITH
The Wind in the Willows BY KENNETH GRAHAME
The Wizard of Oz BY L. FRANK BAUM
This Side of Paradise BY F. SCOTT FITZGERALD
Treasure Island BY ROBERT LOUIS STEVENSON
Ulysses BY JAMES JOYCE
War and Peace BY LEO TOLSTOY
Wuthering Heights BY EMILY BRONTË

www.ingramcontent.com/pod-product-compliance
Lightning Source LLC
Chambersburg PA
CBHW020443100426
42812CB00036B/3435/J